ELEMENTARY TEACHER'S MUSIC ALMANACK:
Timely Lesson Plans for Every Day of the School Year

ELEMENTARY TEACHER'S MUSIC ALMANACK:
Timely Lesson Plans for Every Day of the School Year

Marvin S. Adler

and

Jesse C. McCarroll

Parker Publishing Company, Inc.   West Nyack, New York

Library of Congress Cataloging in Publication Data

Adler, Marvin Stanley.
    Elementary teacher's music almanack.

    1. School music--Instruction and study.
2. Music--Manuals, textbooks, etc. I. McCarroll,
Jesse C.   joint author. II. Title.
MT10.A19   372.8'7'044   78-9138
ISBN 0-13-260836-7

Printed in the United States of America

to MUSIC BELONGS

"Music Alone Shall Live
Never to Die. . . ."

ACKNOWLEDGMENTS

Grateful acknowledgment is hereby made to colleagues in the Humanities Department, New York City Community College (The City University of New York), The Jackie Robinson School of Brooklyn, *Save Music*, and *Music Belongs*. The authors are particularly indebted to the Malverne Public Library and Mrs. Muriel Adler for historical research, to the libraries of Adelphi University and Teachers College, Columbia University for valuable information, to Mark Adler for proofreading and to all those teachers whose continuous flow of ideas make a book such as this possible. We would like to thank the entire faculty of Teachers College, Columbia University for sowing the fertile soil of music education and for being a constant source of inspiration regarding the role of music in our public schools. Finally, we would like to thank the music profession and music industry for their role, in recent years, in saving the concept of "music in the lives of children" from extinction. Without their leadership, we might all—once again—capitulate to the onslaught of the Philistines.

WHAT THIS BOOK CAN DO FOR YOU

Here's an exciting and innovative book for you, the classroom teacher. It will enable you to use ready-made lessons whenever you want to teach music.

We have found that many classroom teachers shy away from music. When faced with the challenge of teaching a music lesson, they feel helpless and inadequate. They feel incapable of teaching music reading, how to sing, or how to play instruments. Often, they feel unable to teach music appreciation, being convinced that there is no way they can get children to enjoy so-called classical music.

This is why an *Elementary Teacher's Music Almanack* is needed. There is a need to take the fear and pain away and to make the teaching experience as easy and enjoyable as possible. There is a need to provide ready-made lesson plans that will enchant and captivate students.

In this book you'll find timely lesson plans that will capitalize upon a multitude of factors: (1) the seasons and holidays of the year; (2) the natural inclination toward popular music; (3) the natural desire to "play" and experiment; (4) the natural pride in cultural heritage; (5) the natural fascination for radio and television commercials; and (6) the natural curiosity about other countries and other people.

Between the covers of this book are hours of musical excitement. Ideas are presented for using music to enhance each day as well as to enrich a variety of other subject areas. Of course, "music for music's sake" is not neglected either; music is explored from every aspect, including listening, singing, creating, interpreting, analyzing, and performing.

Music activities are practical and within the capability of every teacher or child. Both fun-to-do and easy-to-do, each self-contained lesson is tailormade for a particular time of the school year, season, month, day, or holiday. All lessons can be simplified or expanded. All lessons use materials that are either readily available or relatively inexpensive. And they all either capitalize upon children's spontaneity or provide the necessary music and words.

Using this book, you will not have to spend countless hours searching for appropriate materials. All you will need to do is flip the page to the appropriate month, week, or day. Plans proceed chronologically, month by month, from autumn, through Halloween, Thanksgiving, Christmas, New Year's, spring, Easter, May, and June. Interspersed, of course, are relevant plans for ethnic or regional holidays, including Columbus Day, Chanukah, Arbor Day, Black History Week, Hispanic holidays, St. Patrick's Day, and regional celebrations such as the Mardi Gras. Included also are activities to commemorate regional festivities of the many diverse cultures in our society, such as the Quakers, Mormons, Mexican Americans, American Indians, and many others.

Each month features at least one holiday, one special song, one special composer, one special instrument, one special composition, and one special creative experience. These ready-made lesson plans contain many different types of musical activities, not merely singing songs. This is not just another songbook! The primary benefit to you, the elementary classroom teacher, is that any lesson can be used to help bring added joy to any child, either by using music for music's sake or by using music to embellish other subject areas.

We hope that this book helps bring as much musical joy to your classroom as it has to us in the process of preparing it.

Marvin S. Adler

Jesse C. McCarroll

TABLE OF CONTENTS

9

Page   *Lesson Title*   *Activities and Concepts Included*

CHAPTER 4: DECEMBER

CHAPTER 5: JANUARY

CHAPTER 6: FEBRUARY

CHAPTER 7: MARCH

16   CONTENTS

CHAPTER 10: JUNE

1

SEPTEMBER

Children come back to school in September more filled with the excitement of summer than with the desire to begin the hard work of school. Why not capitalize on memories of summer fun? The joys of running, swimming, pets, the zoo, the circus, hiking, trips, and movies can be used to help "ease students into" beginning the school year. We have found that children always love to talk about what they did during the summer. In this chapter you will find some of the many ways that you can combine musical experiences with fond memories of your students' experiences during the vacation. We feel that you'll find many of these activities enjoyable and educational—and easy to teach!

We have also found that students are tremendously excited by new programs on television. After a spring and summer of reruns, children are very happy that new programs are on television. Why not capitalize on this enthusiasm? Television program themes and commercials can be used in the classroom to generate excitement. Through repetition, children know these pieces of music very well. They are often so familiar that they can easily identify them and play theme fragments on a piano or an easy-to-play instrument such as the resonator bells.

Thus, among the lesson plans for September are activities that capitalize on fond memories of the summer and activities that capitalize on the excitement of new television programs. Both types of activity should help you make music come alive in your classroom. We hope that September will be an exciting, musical month for you!

September

Figure 1

Grades: 2-7.

Materials: Chalk and chalkboard or music flash cards.

Concepts:

1. Each letter of the alphabet can open up a world of music.
2. The musical staff, whole notes, and half notes.
3. Highness and lowness of notes.
4. Music notes can have lines that go down on the left side or up on the right side.

**Activities
&
Directions**

1. Place Figure 1 on the board or on music flash cards.
2. Ask the children, "What letter does September begin with?" After getting the answer "S," ask the students to name songs, singers, musical instruments, or anything involved with music that begins with S. Suggest songflute, saxophone, and Schoenberg.
3. Have students guess what the musical notes are in Figure 1 (after the S in September). If they don't guess correctly, tell them to point to the musical E's. Then ask them which musical E is on a line, the upper or lower one. (Answer: the lower one.) Ask them which one is in a space? (Answer: the upper one.) What kinds of notes are the E's? (Answer: half notes.)
4. Have students point to a musical B in Figure 1 and state which line of the staff it is on. (Answer: third or middle.)

5. Distribute paper and have students draw the five lines of the staff, placing musical E's and B's on the staff (from Figure 1).

6. Have students draw E half notes, some with the stems going up on the right side and some with the stems going down on the left side, as in Figure 1. Then have students draw whole note B's.

7. Ask students to describe and differentiate between half and whole notes. Ask them to count the five lines of the musical staff, starting from the bottom, and the four spaces between the lines. Review that whole notes are drawn as circles and do not have stems or vertical lines as half notes do. Review that the E's in Figure 1 are half notes and the B is a whole note. (See Figure 2.)

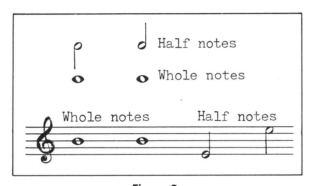

Figure 2

What Did You Do on Vacation?

Grades: K-8.

Materials: Chalk and chalkboard or music flashcards; piano, resonator bells, or Swiss Melode Bells.

Concepts:

1. Ascending C Major scale.
2. Quarter notes.
3. Bar lines.
4. Time signature.
5. 4/4 conducting pattern.

Activities
&
Directions

1. Draw Figure 3 on the chalkboard or on music flash cards. Explain that it shows an ascending C Major scale using quarter notes.

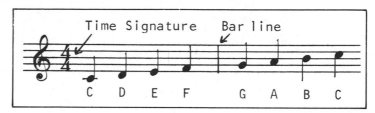

Figure 3

2. Play Figure 3 on the piano or resonator bells.

3. To the scale in Figure 3, sing or chant: "What did you do / on va-ca-tion?"

4. Have students chant answers such as:

    "I went swim-ming / on va-ca-tion."

    "I went to the / zoo one day."

    "I went hi-king / on va-ca-tion."

5. Play the same scale on the Swiss Melode Bells, starting on the letter F instead of C. (F G A B flat C D E F.)

6. Point to the bar line in Figure 3 and explain that bar lines "measure" notes (or separate groups of notes into "measures").

7. Point to the 4/4 time signature and explain that this means four beats in every measure.

8. Point to the quarter notes in Figure 4 and ask children to describe what they look like.

Figure 4

9. Explain that an ascending scale or "ladder of tones" is being used. Explain that the *contour* is going up. The contour could also stay the same, come down, or go up and then come down.

10. Draw Figure 5 (the standard conducting pattern for 4/4) on the chalkboard.

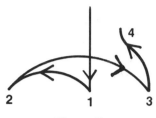

Figure 5

11. Practice the 4/4 conducting pattern with the students.

12. Combine singing (or chanting) with conducting. Use the 4/4 conducting pattern while singing: "What did you do on va - ca - tion?"

13. Have students use the 4/4 conducting pattern as they answer; for example: "I went to the / zoo one day."

Remembrance of Summer Sounds

Grades: 2-6.

Materials: Music that describes different kinds of sound, such as Gershwin's *American in Paris,* Honegger's *Pacific 231,* or Villa-Lobos's *Little Train of the Caipira;* the song "Old Mac-Donald."

Concepts:

1. There are certain sounds we associate with different places that we visit.

2. Many different sounds can be made with the human voice.

**Activities
 &
Directions**

1. Have students describe sounds they have heard while on vacation. You might want to try asking your students to make some of those sounds with their mouths. Many music teachers have found that students love to make mouth pops. Another sound students like to make is the buzz of bees or other insects. We've

had great success in dividing the sounds into "sounds of the city" and "sounds of the woods" so that students can imitate city sirens as well as bird calls.

2. Many teachers have successfully used the song "Old Mac-Donald." When singing the song, use a variety of animal sounds.

3. Ask older children to write short poems describing their summer experiences and the sounds they remember.

4. Listen for the sounds of beeping horns in Gershwin's *American in Paris* and the sound of a train in *Pacific 231* and *Little Train of the Caipira.*

The Circus

Grades: K-4.

Materials: Picture of an elephant; chalk and chalkboard or music flashcards; song "Man on the Flying Trapeze"; recording of *Clown's Dance* by Jacques Ibert or *Circus Band March* by Charles Ives.

Concepts:

1. Slow-moving notes and slow tempo.

2. Half notes.

3. Humorous sounding music is often associated with the circus.

4. Many people perform interesting roles at the circus.

**Activities
&
Directions**

1. Ask children if they were at a circus or the zoo during the summer. You might ask them to bring in snapshots or slides that their parents took.

2. Another enjoyable activity is for the children to describe an elephant. Encourage them to explain the animal's heavy, lumbering gait. We have found that children love to get up and imitate the way an elephant walks.

3. Draw Figure 6 on the chalkboard or on a flashcard. Divide the class into "note pointers" and "elephants." Have the pointers

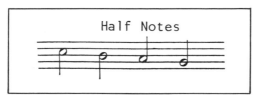

Figure 6

point to the half notes in Figure 6, moving very slowly from one note to another. At the same time, have the students who are the elephants move each time the pointers move to another note. Explain that moving slowly in music is called a slow tempo. Explain that if music is in a slow tempo half notes move slowly.

4. Play *Clown's Dance* or *Circus Band March* and have students play the role of a clown or other people seen at a circus.

5. We have found that students love to draw or trace circus pictures while listening to circus music such as *Clown's Dance*. Students can also describe humorous sounds (sounds they remember themselves or sounds they hear in a composition such as *Circus Band March*).

6. Many music teachers have had great success with the song "Man on the Flying Trapeze." See if your students can complete the first two lines.

> "He flies through the air
> with the greatest of ease,
> The daring young man on the
> ――――― (flying trapeze)

The Zoo

Grades: K-4.

Materials: Saint-Saens' *Carnival of the Animals* or other recordings about animals (such as "Mary Had a Little Lamb").

Concepts:

1. Idea of music describing animals.
2. "Fast" and "slow" in music (tempo).

Activities
   &
Directions

1. Ask the children if they went to a zoo this summer. Discuss what animals they saw. If they saw an elephant, how was it different from those they saw in the circus?

2. Ask the children to describe how some of the zoo animals moved. Encourage them to get up and imitate fast and slow movements of animals that are seen in a zoo but are not generally seen at a circus. Try to tie this in with a discussion of fast and slow tempos in music (the tempo is the speed of the music).

3. Ask students to bring recordings about animals to school. Supplement the recordings they bring to school with Saint-Saens' *Carnival of the Animals* or "Mary Had a Little Lamb."

4. You might want to try to develop the vocabulary word "tempo." Each time a student says "a fast beat," replace "beat" with "tempo." Another enjoyable activity is for students to draw (pictures or musical notes) while listening to the recordings.

Camping

Grades: 5-8.

Materials: Recordings of Frederick Delius' *Summer Night on the River* and Felix Mendelssohn's *A Midsummer Night's Dream;* sheet-music for the song "Valderi" (also called "The Happy Wanderer").

Concepts:

1. Many famous composers have written music about the summer.

2. Many people enjoy camping while on a summer vacation.

Activities
   &
Directions

1. Students who camped out during the summer should be encouraged to share their experiences with the class.

2. Have students who camped near water describe their night experiences with the class. Then play *Summer Night on the River.*

3. Tell students that Mendelssohn was only 17 years old when he composed *A Midsummer Night's Dream.* Discuss how the work is based on the work of the same name by Shakespeare and that it is "incidental music," a composition for orchestra associated with a specific drama. We've found that students enjoy learning that 19th Century composers frequently wrote music for dramas, to be played at the beginning of the play and in between the acts. Another enjoyable activity is to have students listen to classical radio stations to try to hear different examples of incidental music. Many music teachers have found that it is worthwhile to compare the styles of *A Midsummer Night's Dream* and other incidental music.

4. Place Figure 7 on the board or on flashcards and then listen to or sing "Valderi" (The Happy Wanderer"). See page 194.

Figure 7

Clouds

Grades: K-8.

Materials: Recording of "Cloudburst" from *Grand Canyon Suite* by Ferde Grofe; recording of Johnny Ray singing "Little White Cloud that Cried" (or a similar song about clouds); recording of *Nuages* (Clouds) by Claude Debussy.

Concepts:

1. Both songs and classical compositions have been written about clouds.

2. Clouds can be sung about or described musically.

Activities
&
Directions

1. Have children go to the window and look at clouds in the sky. Ask them if during the summer they enjoyed watching the clouds while they were in the park or the woods. You might want to ask them to draw clouds on plain paper or to make tiny clouds that act as notes on music paper (see Figure 8).

Figure 8

2. Play one of the recordings about clouds and see how it affects the children. Does it relax them? Put them to sleep? Make them draw better? Many music teachers have found that the impressionistic music of Debussy helps relax many children. You might also want to try showing impressionistic paintings of clouds or paintings of clouds from other periods of art. The children can also be told that one sees clouds at night too and that the Debussy piece about clouds is actually a *nocturne* ("night piece").

Rain

Grades: 2-8.

Materials: Chalk and chalkboard or music flashcards; recordings of "Raindrops Keep Falling on My Head," "Soon It's Gonna Rain," "Constant Rain," "Laughter in the Rain," or "I'm Singing in the Rain."

Concepts:

1. Music skips down and up.
2. The *interval* in music.
3. The "minor third" interval.

**Activities
  &
Directions**

1. Ask pupils what they did during the summer when it rained (watched movies? television?). Try to get your students to talk about how the rain made them feel—especially if they were anxious to go swimming.

2. Place Figure 9 on the chalkboard or on music flashcards. Point to the notes while singing them, first using words, then solfeggio (*do, re, mi*), and then the numbers. Explain that the distance between two notes in music is called the interval, and that the interval is measured by counting the number of tones between two notes, the starting tone inclusive. Finally, ask the students what the name of the song is. (Answer: "It's Raining It's Pouring.")

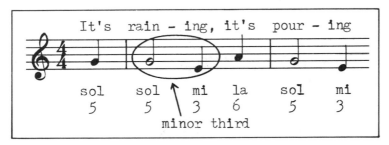

Figure 9

3. Tell students that the name of the interval between the second and third tones in Figure 9 is a "minor third," one of the most common intervals in folksongs. We have had great success in having students remember the "minor third" interval for long periods of time through this song. You might also want to ask them if they can think of other songs that use it.

4. Listen to recorded examples of other songs about rain (see "Materials").

Storms and Hurricanes

Grades: 3-8.

Materials: Recordings of the "Hurricane Scene" from Gershwin's *Porgy and Bess* and the song "Stormy Weather."

Concepts:

1. Dissonances in music.
2. Tone clusters.
3. Musical thunder can be created by using two- or three-note dissonances at the lower end of the piano (left-hand side) or by using full-handed tone clusters.

Activities
&
Directions

1. Many children are terrified during thunder and lightning storms (some adults are, too); use this as a way of thinking back on the summer. Were there any storms your children can remember that frightened them? Ask the children to remember the thunder and the lightning.

2. Many music teachers have found that notes played very close together at the lower left-hand side of the piano sound like thunder to children. Ask your students if notes played that way sound like thunder to them. Explain that notes played very close together create *dissonances* in music. These dissonances are created by irregular sound vibrations. Explain also that very deep pitches in music have low frequencies. You might also want to try having students come up to the piano to play this "musical thunder." First tell them to play two notes at a time. Then have them play three. Then have them place their whole hands down for "tone clusters." Teach them to respond to the word "thunder" by playing tone clusters. Many teachers have found that children love this activity. They also love contrasting the sound with light tinkling at the extreme right-hand side of the piano, which can be called "rain." Older students, by the way, can be told that Charles Ives and Henry Cowell were among the American composers first to use tone clusters in compositions.

3. Play other compositions about storms and hurricanes, such as "Stormy Weather" and the "Hurricane Scene" from the Gershwin opera *Porgy and Bess.* Have students listen for sounds of human voices and instruments representing wind, thunder, and lightning. See if any students get frightened. The portion

of Ferde Grofe's *Grand Canyon Suite* entitled "Cloudburst" can also be used here.

4. Additional discussion can be obtained by asking your students what happens to people who live near a large river when it floods due to a severe summer storm. Or you might want to discuss how hurricanes are formed in the ocean, thus relating a music lesson with science. You can also have students create poems about storms in the sea and then compare them to poems about the sea by Walt Whitman. Ask students why a composer such as Ernest Bloch actually entitled his musical composition *Poems of the Sea*?

Souvenirs

Grades: 2-8.

Materials: Recordings of *Souvenir de Porto Rico* by Louis Moreau Gottschalk, the "Waltz" from *Souvenirs* by Samuel Barber, and *Souvenir de Florence*, Op. 70, by Tchaikovsky.

Concepts:

1. Many people visit different cities and countries during their summer vacations.

2. Souvenirs help people remember the different places they visit.

Activities & Directions

1. Ask students to obtain souvenirs of special things that are found in their own city, town, or state. You might want to try having the children design and create souvenirs of famous places. Many teachers have found that this is an enjoyable activity, and we've had considerable success with this approach. Others have found, however, that it is just as well to have children bring in souvenirs that their parents have kept from their trips.

2. Listen to one or more of the recordings listed in "Materials." You might want to point out that both Tchaikovsky and

Gottschalk were 19th Century composers. Gottschalk was American and Tchaikovsky was Russian. You might also want to point out that Barber is a 20th Century American composer. Tell the children that a waltz is in 3/4 time and that Gottschalk's composition has much "syncopation" (displacing of music's normal accents).

Dogs, Cats, and Other Pets

Grades: K-5.

Materials: Chalk and chalkboard or music flashcards; recordings of songs about pets or songs about animals, such as "How Much Is That Doggie in the Window?" and "We Are Siamese if You Please."

Concepts:

1. Songs are written about pets.
2. Among the different types of music are "descriptive" and "pure," or "absolute," music.
3. 3/4 meter and waltz time.
4. Sharps (#).

Activities
&
Directions

1. Ask children if they played with their pets this summer, or if they bought a new cat, dog, turtle, or other animal.
2. Play recordings of "How Much Is That Doggie in the Window?" "We Are Siamese if You Please," or any record about a pet that is applicable.
3. Place Figure 10 on the chalkboard or on flashcards. Explain

Figure 10

that this song ("How Much Is That Doggie in the Window?") is a waltz and is in 3/4 meter.

4. Point to the first five notes of "How Much Is That Doggie in the Window?" and sing: *sol, do, sol, mi, do.* Point to and explain the F sharp (F#) on the first or bottom space of the staff.

Running

Grades: K-3.

Materials: Chalk and chalkboard or music flashcards; musical toys.

Concepts:

1. Sixteenth notes.
2. Fast *tempo.*

**Activities
&
Directions**

1. List some summer activities that involve walking and some that involve running. Discuss speed and point out that running is faster than walking. Let this lead up to your pointing out that in music some notes are fast and others are slow, that a whole note is fairly slow and sixteenth notes move rather quickly.

2. Place Figure 11 on the chalkboard or on flashcards. Point to and distinguish between the sixteenth notes and the whole note.

Figure 11

3. Have children run when you point to the sixteenth notes and walk when you point to the whole note. We've found that children enjoy this activity very much, and many teachers have claimed success with such a procedure in developing the concept of fast versus slow.

Swimming

Grades: 3-6.

Materials: Lined composition paper; recordings of any songs about water; recording of Claude Debussy's *La Mer* (The Sea) or Frederick Delius's *Sea Drift*.

Concepts:

1. Music enhances the pleasure of any activity, even one already as enjoyable as swimming.
2. Musical variety is often craved when one is listening to music for a long time.

Activities
&
Directions

1. Try to develop a lively debate as to where it is better to swim, in a pool, in a lake, or at the beach. See if there are any musical reasons why some may prefer one over the other. (For example, at a pool you don't get sand on or in an expensive radio or cassette tape player).
2. Ask students who went to the beach a lot during the summer if they remember a lot of different musical styles on radios that people brought to the beach. Try to develop a discussion about the importance of musical diversity. Try to get students to want to write about it on paper.
3. Ask students who went to a lake to swim whether there was a loudspeaker with music being played. Ask them if they remember what was usually played over the loudspaker. Was there an assortment of popular music, classical music, and jazz? Ask the same questions of students who went to a pool most of the time. Try to get the lake and pool swimmers to write about the types of music or specific songs that were played over the loudspeakers.
4. Play *La Mer* by Debussy or *Sea Drift* by Delius for your students. You might want to try to have them imagine the water, lying on a beach, sailing on a boat, or sitting on a porch near the water. Another enjoyable activity is for the children to close their eyes and use swimming motions when they feel like it.

Take Me Out to the Ballgame

Grades: 3-7.

Materials: Chalk and chalkboard or music flashcards; resonator bells; baseball bat.

Concepts:

1. 3/4 meter.
2. Accent.
3. Octave.
4. Transposition.

Activities
&
Directions

1. Place Figure 12 on the chalkboard or on music flashcards. Play the song on the resonator bells to show the children how the tune goes and then sing "Take me/ out to the/ ball/ game" while pointing to the notes. You might want to stop at this point and ask your students about their summer and how often they played baseball. Or you might wish to continue by having the children sing the same four measures, reminding them that the bar lines separate the beats into measures and that the rhythmic names are half, quarter/ quarter, quarter, quarter/ dotted-half/ dotted-half.

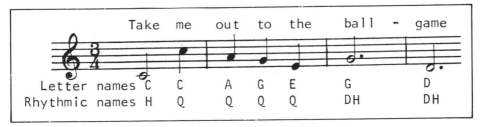

Figure 12

2. Explain that the jump up from middle C to high C is called an octave and that the octave is an interval of eight steps between the two notes (counting the bottom note: C is 1, D is 2, E is 3, F is 4, G is 5, A is 6, B is 7, and C is 8).

3. Divide the class into bell players, singers, "swingers," conductors, and note pointers. Play a game in which the "swingers" have to swing a baseball bat when the bell players, singers, and note pointers get to the word "ball," swinging forward on the word "ball" and back on the word "game." While the singers, pointers, and swingers do their thing, you can have the "conductors" conduct the standard 3/4 pattern (see Figure 13). We have found that children love to "conduct" music, and this song has been used successfully in teaching the concept of 3/4 meter (three beats in a measure). The concept of *accent* is also made clear by the movement of the bat on the word "ball."

$\frac{3}{4}$ **conducting pattern**

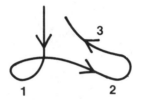

Figure 13

4′ 33″

At the beginning of the year, all teachers want to train a class to be quiet when necessary. The piece *4′ 33″* (a composition by the American composer John Cage) can be both a game and an experience that will help develop listening skills and the concept of chance music.

Grades: K-8.

Materials: None.

Concepts:

1. Chance, or aleatoric, music.
2. Rests and silence in music.

**Activities
&
Directions**

1. Explain to the children that in the first performance of *4′ 33″* the pianist came on to the stage, but instead of playing the

piano, just sat there for *4' 33"*. Explain that the idea was to highlight the importance of silence, and also that silence really contains many sounds.

2. To demonstrate how many sounds there are in silence, perform *4' 33"*. Tell the children to be absolutely quiet when you say "Now." Then, using a clock or a stopwatch, try to make no sounds for the necessary length of time. But ask the students to listen for the sounds you begin hearing when you try to be very quiet. Discuss sounds such as those of birds, a clock ticking, a radiator making noise, or sounds of voices from another room.

What's New on Television?

Grades: 3-8.

Materials: Cassette tape recorder; blank cassette cartridge.

Concepts:

1. Musical identification.
2. Theme recognition.

Activities
&
Directions

1. After a summer of "reruns" on television, students are sometimes glad to welcome the fall. The fall brings with it all the new television programs that children will be watching all year. You might want to try the following lesson, which capitalizes on this enthusiasm. Ask your students to list their favorite new television programs of the season, with the appropriate days, times, and channels.

2. Record the opening musical themes of the television programs the children listed. Bring the tape you made to school and play it for your students. Ask the children if they recognize the musical themes. You might want to have them raise their hands and tell you what the themes are. Or you might have them come up to the board to write down the names of the programs. Some teachers prefer to distribute paper and have the students make columns, such as,

---

#1   TELEVISION PROGRAM   DAY   CHANNEL

To lead up to a writing assignment, you might want to take the following approach. After the students' initial excitement of hearing the music from some of their favorite programs, ask students if they are willing to "test" themselves on paper. If so, have them number 1 through 10 or 20 (depending on how many themes you have recorded). Then play one theme at a time and have the students write down the program name, the day and time, and the channel.

COMPOSERS OF THE MONTH

Happy Birthday Arnold Schoenberg
(September 13)

Grades: 2-8.

Materials: Chalk and chalkboard; recording of *Pierrot Lunaire,* Opus 21, by Schoenberg (optional).

Concepts:

1. Any day might be the birthday of a great composer of music.
2. Schoenberg was the founder of 12 note or 12 tone music (one of the major styles of 20th Century music).

**Activities
&
Directions**

1. On the chalkboard write:

   HAPPY BIRTHDAY ARNOLD SCHOENBERG
   (September 13, 1874)

2. To tie in with mathematics, ask your students how many years ago Schoenberg was born. How many years after Antonin Dvorak (born 1824) was Schoenberg born? (Answer: 50.)
3. Sing "Happy Birthday" to Arnold Schoenberg.
4. Write 1, 2, 3, 4, 5, 6, 7, 8, 9, 10, 11, 12 on the board.

5. Rather than confuse students with an elaborate explanation of 12 tone music, simply tell students that there are 12 different notes in 12 tone music. (For grades 6-8, you can explain that the 12 tones are the 12 different notes in the octave. Compute how many different melodies one can get by multiplying 12 × 12, times about 20 different kinds of note values. (A: 2,880)

6. If you have a recording, play parts of *Pierrot Lunaire*. Tell students that it is a story about moonsickness. See if you can motivate a lively discussion of the occult—or at least a discussion of moonmadness and werewolves.

Happy Birthday George Gershwin
(September 26)

Grades: 2-8.

Materials: Chalk and chalkboard; auto horn; recordings of *Porgy and Bess* and *An American in Paris* or *Rhapsody in Blue*.

Concepts:

1. Any day might be the birthday of a great composer of music.
2. George Gershwin was among the first to combine classical music and jazz sounds.

**Activities
&
Directions**

1. On the chalkboard write:
   HAPPY BIRTHDAY GEORGE GERSHWIN
   (September 26, 1898)
   Ask children how many dozen years after Schoenberg George Gershwin was born? (Answer: 1898 minus 1874 is 24 or two dozen.)

2. Sing "Happy Birthday George Gershwin."

3. Listen to *An American in Paris* and look at pictures or slides of Paris. Beep small horns when they are used in the music. Listen to excerpts from *Porgy and Bess*. Listen to the famous clarinet solo at the beginning of *Rhapsody in Blue*.

2

OCTOBER

Children sometimes come to school in October with their minds more filled with thoughts of football, falling leaves, and Halloween than with the everyday business of school. But the music period can utilize these interests to make school fun as well as educational. For most children, even if they have to rake leaves October is a fun-filled month that includes "trick or treating" in cheerful costumes. You can capitalize on these exciting aspects of October and bring them into the classroom—as creative teachers have always done! In this chapter you will find some of the many ways that you can combine musical experiences with the joyful anticipation of being out on the football field, romping in piles of leaves, and "trick or treating."

We have found that when adults begin to complain about those first chills of autumn, young people take on a new vigor, start forgetting about how "terrible" it is to be back in school, and vitalize adults with their new-found enthusiasm. Just mention Halloween to your students, and you'll see their eyes light up—especially if you get on the subject of witches, goblins, skeletons, and black cats. Just take out a football, and you'll see your students take on new energy.

October is also a time when tastes are being consolidated as to which television programs your students like best. This interest in the fall season schedule of programs can also be used in the classroom to generate excitement. Just as you asked the children "What's new on television?" in September, you can now ask your students "What have you been watching on television?" Interest can thus be used to develop concepts of perceptive listening and musical identification. Particular program themes should now be well known, and the music for particular commercials should be thoroughly familiar. Theme recognition can thus be the central concept of one or more listening lessons.

October

Figure 14

Grades: 2-7.

Materials: Chalk and chalkboard or music flashcards.

Concepts:

1. Quarter, whole, and half notes.
2. Octaves.
3. The music staff.

**Activities
  &
Directions**

1. Place Figure 14 on the chalkboard or music flashcards. Have your students copy Figure 14. Ask them to identify the letter names of the music notes. (Answers: C, B, and E.) You might also ask your students if they can identify the rhythmic *values* of C, B, and E. The correct answers are:

    C—quarter notes
    B—whole note
    E—half notes

2. Another enjoyable way of using Figure 14 is for students to come to the board or the posted flashcards. You might have the children point to the figure O C T O B E R, placing their fingers on the letters *and* the music notes as they say: "O, C, T, O, B, E, R." Or you can teach the children to say:

    O
    C   quarter notes
    T
    O
    B   whole note
    E   half notes
    R

3. Explain the "double notes" as representing the concept of the octave, duplication of a tone eight notes higher (such as CDEFGABC). Of course remind students that there is no H in American music and that A comes after G (when adjacent).

Falling Leaves

Grades: 3-5.

Materials: Chalk and chalkboard; leaves; music flashcards.

Concepts:

1. Whole, half, and quarter notes.
2. Learning music notes can be fun.

**Activities
 &
Directions**

1. Place Figure 15 on the chalkboard or music flashcards.

Figure 15

2. Have students copy Figure 15.
3. Call for students who can name the musical notes in Figure 15 by letter name and note or rhythmic value. (Answers: F whole notes, A half note, G quarter notes in the word F A L L I N G; E whole notes, A half note, E quarter notes in the word L E A V E S.)

4. Place music flash cards on the floor in front of the room. Ask students who have brought some of the dried leaves of autumn to school to come forward, and ask them to try to drop them on the flashcards and identify the lines or spaces of the treble staff on which they fall. (See Figure 16.)

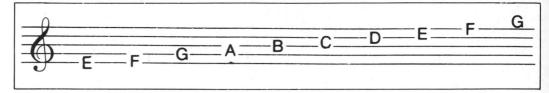

Figure 16

Autumn Leaves

Grades: 2-6.

Materials: Autumn leaves; recording of the song "Autumn Leaves" or the German folk tune "Autumn Leaves Now Are Falling"; recording of Chopin's Fantasie Impromptu in C Sharp Minor.

Concepts:

1. Downward motion is called *descending,* and both leaves and musical scales can descend.

2. When leaves loose their chlorophyll, they turn orange or red. This usually happens late in September or early in October.

Activities
&
Directions

1. Children love to make a display of leaves from different kinds of trees or draw leaves on construction paper. Why not have them display either type of artwork on a bulletin board? As the children work, you can play a recording of "Autumn Leaves" or "Autumn Leaves Now Are Falling."

2. You might want also want to play Chopin's Fantasie Impromptu in C Sharp Minor as background music for working with autumn leaves. There are sections in which there are de-

scending, chromatic notes. During these sections children can let some leaves slowly drop to the floor. Another fun activity during these descending, chromatic passages is for the children to use their hands and their bodies to dramatize the descent of the notes. Try to contrast these sections with passages in which the music ascends.

Autumn

Grades: 4-8.

Materials: A recording of "Autumn" from *The Four Seasons* by Vivaldi or a recording of "Autumn" from *The Seasons* by Alexander Glazunov.

Concepts:

1. Music can describe the seasons of the year.
2. Music differs as to speed (*tempo*) and the instruments that are used (*orchestration*).

Activities
&
Directions

1. Play either the Vivaldi or the Glazunov recording and ask your students whether the section on "Autumn" actually describes autumn. Children can be very creative in the way they listen, so be sure to keep an open mind. However, be prepared also to direct their listening. You might call their attention to anything that sounds like strong winds or dancing leaves being driven around by a strong gust.

2. Another way to listen is to call your students' attention to differences in tempo (the speed of the music) or the instrumentation (the instruments that are used). Children may want to see pictures of any instruments you mention, so it might be helpful to have a book of pictures nearby.

3. As children listen to the music about autumn, they may want to write poems or make up stories. We have found that this is a very worthwhile activity and one that children enjoy very much.

Black Cats

Grades: K-4.

Materials: Chalk and chalkboard; music flashcards; rubber toy cats; Magic Marker.

Concepts:

1. Whole notes.
2. Treble clef sign.
3. Learning music notes can be fun.

**Activities
&
Directions**

1. Place Figure 17 on the chalkboard or on music flashcards. Point to the notes and letters of the figure, placing your fingers first on the letters of the alphabet and then on the musical notes as well, saying: "B, L, A, C, K C, A, T, S." We have had marvelous success at getting children's attention by using small, rubber toy cats. You might try placing them right over the whole notes B, A, and C. If you are good at drawing, you might also try drawing small cats in place of the whole notes themselves.

Figure 17

2. Point to the treble clef sign (see Figure 18). Ask your pupils if the bottom twist looks like the tail of a cat. Compare it with the tail of the rubber toy cats you have. You might want to show your class how to draw the treble clef, or you might want to "play" with the drawing by adding whiskers or eyes!

Figure 18

3. Distribute music flash cards and have students draw black cats on lines and spaces of the staff, trying to get them to draw the cats either *in a space* or *on a line.*

Columbus Day

Grades: 1-5.

Materials: Toy boats; boats made from folded paper; cut-out cardboard boats; five pieces of 4-foot-long string; music flashcards; chalk and chalkboard.

Concepts:

1. Knowledge of lines and spaces of the treble staff.
2. Learning notation can be fun.

Activities
&
Directions

1. Children love to play games. One game that we have used successfully centers around using toy boats to learn notation. First, call for three of the toy boats that children have brought to class and name them *Nina, Pinta,* and *Santa Maria.* Next, spread the five pieces of string out on the floor, parallel to each other and three inches apart. Place the *Nina* in the second space from the bottom, as in Figure 19. Starting with the *Nina* in the A space, ask one child to "sail" the *Nina* up through A, B, C, D, E, F, G, moving from the second space to the third line, to the third space, and so on up to G above the staff. As the boat "sails" upward, you might from time to time say "stop" and ask what note the boat is on.

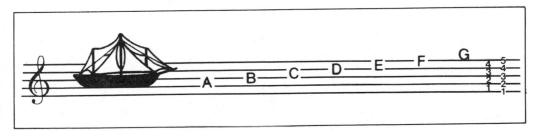

Figure 19

2. Repeat the game with the *Pinta,* calling on different children. Then play the game with the *Santa Maria,* using still other pupils. You might also have other children go to the board, draw five lines with chalk, and then "sail" cut-out boats up the staff from the second space A up through G—going systematically from A in the second space to B on the third line, to C in the third space, to D on the fourth line, to E in the fourth space, to F on the fifth line, to G above the staff.

3. Another enjoyable variation on the game using "Columbus' boats" to teach the musical alphabet is as follows. Use masking tape to place music flashcards on the walls all around the room. You can then have many children "sailing" paper or toy boats from A through G. Children can be told: "Now sail only in the A space," "Now sail in only the C space," "Now sail on only the B line," and so on.

4. Ask your students what letter of the *musical alphabet* is common to the words *Nina, Pinta,* and *Santa Maria.* (Answer: A.) To reinforce this concept, you might return to "sailing" only in the A space for a while.

5. As background listening, you might play music such as the "Venetian Boat Songs" from *Songs Without Words* by Felix Mendelssohn, or you might play more popular Italian songs such as "Arrivederci Roma" or "Volare." You might also dance the lively *tarantella*!

Football Frolic
(Musical Footballs #1)

Grades: K-6.

Materials: Five pieces of four-foot-long string; chalk and chalkboard; a football.

Concepts:

1. Lines and spaces of the staff.
2. Correct way of writing music.

**Activities
 &
Directions**

1. Stretch five pieces of string out over the floor, parallel to each other and eight inches apart (so that it looks like a musical

staff). Tape the string down so that it can't move. Place a foot-ball on the bottom string and then move it up so that it is in between the bottom string and the second string (see Figure 20). Teachers who have used this game have found that students love to come to the front of the room and move the football from the bottom string to in between the bottom and second strings—and so forth until the football has been on every string and in every space. You might also point out to the students that correctly written musical notes look more like footballs than like basketballs.

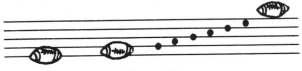

Figure 20

2. Another enjoyable variant of this game involves taping the pieces of string to the chalkboard or bulletin board. Hold the football in the second space (see Figure 21) and explain that this space is called "A." Move the ball up to the middle line and explain that it is "B." Move the ball between the middle string and fourth string and call it "C." Move the ball to the fourth string and call it "D." Move the ball between the fourth and top strings and call it "E." Move the ball to the top string and call it "F." Finally, move the ball on the top string and call it "G." You have just gone through the musical alphabet: A, B, C, D, E, F, G.

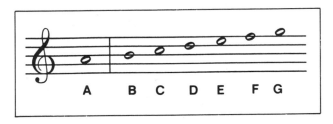

Figure 21

More Football Frolic
(Musical Footballs #2)

Grades: 3-7.

Materials: Chalk and chalkboard; music pen; printed music.

Concepts:

    1. Drawing whole notes.

    2. Drawing music properly.

**Activities
&
Directions**

    1. Draw a football on the board and ask students to identify it. Now ask students to draw a picture of a football between two pieces of string. Explain that musical whole notes look more like footballs or eggs when drawn properly than like tennis balls (see Figure 22).

CORRECT   **INCORRECT**

Figure 22

    2. Using a single line, demonstrate that "line notes" are drawn above and below the line (see Figure 23). Refer back to Figure 22 to see how "space notes" are drawn in between two lines.

Figure 23

    3. Children will love it if you go around the room to each student and, using a music pen, individually draw "musical footballs" or whole notes for each student. You might, if time permits, draw two whole notes for each child, a line note and a space note. (See Figure 24.)

Figure 24

What Have You Been Watching on Television?

Grades: 3-8.

Materials: Chalk and chalkboard; paper; copies of television guides (*T.V. Guide* or from the newspaper); cassette tape recorder; blank tape cartridge.

Concepts:

1. Effectiveness of background music.
2. Musical identification.
3. Theme recognition.

**Activities
   &
Directions**

1. If you have already used the September lesson "What's New on Television," ask students if they have changed their minds about their favorite television programs of the season. If they have changed their minds, try to obtain a lively discussion of why, especially asking if the music had anything to do with their change of feeling. Elicit comments about how music creates excitement. Have children argue about which background themes are better than others. Get children to sing, whistle, or clap the rhythms of some of their new favorites.

2. If you have *not* used the September lesson "What's New on Telvision," ask children to bring television guides to class. Have them circle their favorite programs, particularly ones with musical excitement. Collect these television guides and, using a cassette tape, record the musical themes or background music of the television programs the students listed.

3. Back in the classroom, play the cassette tapes you made for your students and ask them if they can recognize the themes and if they can identify the television programs represented by the themes.

4. After the initial excitement has died down (especially if your students are well motivated), ask students if they are willing to "test" themselves on paper. If so, ask them to number 1 through 10 or 20 (depending upon how many television

themes you have). Then play one musical theme at a time, having students write down the name of the television program from which the theme comes. (Optional: test students' ability to recall the day, time, and channel of the programs from which the themes come.)

Octoberfest

Grades: 2-5.

Materials: Chalk and chalkboard; German (preferably Bavarian) style folk dress; recordings of, or music for, German folk songs or polkas.

Concepts:

1. A polka is a two-beat-per-measure, "duple" time, or 2/4 type of music.

2. October is the German festival month known as Octoberfest.

Activities
&
Directions

1. Show children pictures of the type of dress worn in an Octoberfest celebration. Ask them to try to obtain such clothing for a class celebration.

2. On the day chosen for the children to come to school in the German folk dress, have a phonograph set up to play German polkas or folk songs such as "Ach du Lieber Augenstein." After doing a few polkas or, if necessary, teaching the children how to dance the polka, explain that a polka is a type of dance that has a strong ONE two/ ONE two/ ONE two beat. Write 2/4 on the board and explain that this means ONE two/ ONE two/ ONE two, or two beats in every measure.

3. Sing "Ach du Lieber Augenstein" or a similar German folksong that many children know. Explain that many German folksongs (such as "Ach du Lieber Augenstein") have a very strong downbeat. Use your fist to demonstrate the emphasis given to the first beat.

October Tubafest

Grades: 2-7.

Materials: Recording of *Tubby the Tuba;* pictures of the tuba and the sousaphone; a record player.

Concepts:

1. The tuba and the sousaphone are among the lowest or deepest sounding instruments of the orchestra.
2. Pitch means highness or lowness of sound.

Activities
&
Directions

1. Play a recording of *Tubby the Tuba* (which children in the lower grades should find particularly amusing). Ask them questions such as: When was Tubby very unhappy? Why and when did Tubby become happy? You might even want to assign roles to some of your students and re-enact portions of this delightful composition. Many music teachers have found that this is a sound "action" approach.

2. Show pictures of the tuba and comment on how big it is. You can then explain "pitch" as highness and lowness of sound and as being related to the length of the instrument. Jokingly tell them this is why the tiny piccolo is so high pitched.

3. There have been tuba orchestras for many years in other parts of the world, but tuba orchestras are a fairly recent occurrence in United States music education. You might try asking your students to imagine the sound of a 60-member orchestra of tubas. Ask them if they have ever seen a tubafest. If you can obtain a recording of a tuba orchestra, play it for your class. Discuss the type of music such an orchestra is best suited to play (waltzes, polkas, and marches). Children will also love doing these dances. If you can teach them to your students, it is a very enjoyable activity.

Halloween

Grades: 2-7.

Materials: Recordings such as *Danse Macabre* by Saint Saens, *Hallowe'en* by Charles Ives, *Songs and Dances of Death* by Rachmaninoff, "Witches' Ride" from *Hansel and Gretel* by Humperdink, and "Dream of a Witches' Sabbath" from *Symphonie Fantastique* by Hector Berlioz.

Concepts:

1. Halloween has inspired many composers to write music.
2. Witches, ghosts, and skeletons—as well as the traditional pumpkin—are among the many things associated with Halloween.
3. On Halloween children love to scare each other and go "trick or treating."

**Activities
&
Directions**

1. You might start out by discussing Halloween in general, asking your students if they are going to do the usual "trick or treating." Let this lead into a more general discussion of how Halloween came about and the things associated with it, such as bones, skeletons, and other scary things. Tell them there are some musical compositions that are both fun and scary, such as *Danse Macabre*. Play the opening of *Danse Macabre* and point out that the music starts with twelve strokes that represent midnight. See if children can discover which instrument represents bones rattling. (Answer: the xylophone.) Ask your students if the music sounds frightening and if they enjoy scary music. You might find the poem "Danse Macabre" by Henri Cazalis and read it as the music is being played. You might also have the children write their own poems as the music is being played. Another technique that works well is to compare this composition with others, such as *Hallowe'en* by Charles Ives, the "Witches' Ride" by Humperdinck, and the "Dream of a Witches' Sabbath" by Berlioz.
2. Another enjoyable activity for Halloween involves drawing or

using construction paper to make jack-o'-lanterns, masks, and skeletons. We've had great success with such an approach. For example, you can play "Witches' Ride" or "Dream of a Witches' Sabbath" and have children draw a witch on a broomstick. You can play *Danse Macabre* and have children move about the room with the skeletons they made, acting out getting out of the graves, dancing around, and then returning to the graves! Children love this! You can also shut out all the lights in the room and place a lit candle in a jack-o'-lantern. In such an atmopshere, a composition such as *Songs and Dances of Death* is twice as frightening!

3. Many music teachers have found that Berlioz's *Symphonie Fantastique* is one of the best works to demonstrate the concept of program music. You can tell your students that this symphony differs from most of those that come before it in that the entire symphony tells a story and follows a plot. In fact, one of the leading characters has her own "tune," called an *idee fix,* which appears whenever she comes into the story. Thus, the movement entitled "Dream of a Witches' Sabbath" can be used to teach music history—especially of the 19th century, which is when Berlioz lived.

COMPOSERS OF THE MONTH

Happy Birthday Saint-Saens
(October 9)

Grades: 2-7.

Materials: Recordings of *Wedding Cake,* "The Swan" from *Carnival of the Animals,* and the Clarinet Concerto by Saint-Saens; record player; pictures of the clarinet and the cello; pictures of swans.

Concepts:

1. An instrumental *solo* features one instrument.

2. The clarinet is a single-reed instrument and a member of the woodwind family of instruments. The cello is a string instrument much larger than the violin or viola but smaller than the double bass.

**Activities
&
Directions**

1. On the board, write:

   HAPPY BIRTHDAY CAMILLE SAINT-SAENS
   (October 9, 1835)

   and explain that the proper pronunciation of Saint-Saens is
   San Sahns. If children are curious about the name, this might
   be a good time to ask them to guess what country Saint-Saens
   was from. (Answer: France.) You can also go right into a
   routine tie-in with mathematics, asking your students to figure
   out how many years ago Saint-Saens was born. You might want
   to try singing Happy Birthday in a slow waltz time (3/4 meter)
   and have your students move their arms as if they were swans.
   This is particularly successful in the lower grades and is good
   preparation for listening to Saint-Saens' "The Swan."

2. When listening to "The Swan," you might find it effective to
   show pictures of swans and the cello, which is the solo instrument. You might discuss the silky sound of the cello or its
   relationship in size to the violin, viola, and bass viol. You might
   ask the children to imagine the swan gliding in a lake. If you
   draw well, draw a picture of a swan or a cello on the board. If
   your students have good imaginations, ask them to think of the
   cello magically becoming a swan, and vice versa.

3. Another composition by Saint-Saens that might appeal to children is *Wedding Cake.* As you and your class listen to the music,
   you can look at wedding pictures, discuss weddings you've
   been to, partake of some cake that a generous parent has
   baked for the occasion, or act out a wedding scene right in your
   classroom! We have found that children love to be brides and
   grooms, especially in the second through fourth grades. You
   might even want to try throwing rice at the newly married
   couple!

4. We have found that children are fascinated by the fact that
   Saint-Saens was 86 years old when he wrote his Clarinet Concerto. For this reason, many music teachers use the composition in their teaching. Related activities can be: looking at pictures of the clarinet, explaining that a concerto is a classical
   composition that features a solo instrument, comparing a solo
   cello with a solo clarinet, and speculating why Camille Saint-
   Saens never wrote a clarinet concerto before he was 86.

Salt Peanuts
(October 21)

Grades: 2-8.

Materials: Bags of salted peanuts; recording of "Salt Peanuts" by "Dizzy" Gillespie; pictures of "Dizzy" Gillespie; chalk and chalkboard or music flashcards.

Concepts:

1. Awareness of the type of jazz down as *bop* or *be-bop*.
2. Visual and aural perception of the musical interval, the octave.

Activities
&
Directions

1. On the chalkboard, write:
   ### HAPPY BIRTHDAY DIZZY GILLESPIE
   (October 21, 1917)

   Sing Happy Birthday to Dizzy in a "jazzy" way, perhaps dressed up with dark glasses and French berets, as the be-boppers did in the late 1940's and early 1950's. Ask your students to figure out how many years ago, and in what country, Dizzy Gillespie was born. (He was born in the United States.) As a tie-in with history, ask older students if they can think of what happened in United States history in 1917, the year of Dizzy Gillespie's birth. (Answer: The United States entered World War I.)

2. As preparation for playing a recording or tape of "Salt Peanuts," tell your students that whenever they hear the words "Salt Peanuts, Salt Peanuts" they should stand up and place four peanuts in their mouths. Then distribute small bags of salted peanuts to your surprised and delighted students! Now place Figure 25 on the chalkboard or on music flashcards. You might point to the notes in Figure 25 whenever the recording gets to the part where the musicians sing "Salt Peanuts, Salt Peanuts" and explain that the musical leaps or skips here use the interval of an octave (notes that are eight tones apart). A physical (or manipulative) way of developing this concept of the octave is as follows. Have children go to the piano and count up from the bottom A. (Note: A is the lowest note on the

Figure 25

piano.) Have them count A, B, C, D, E, F. Then have them count up F, G, A, B, C, D, E, F, and have them place the right index finger on the higher F. Now, you might see if any of your students can play and sing:

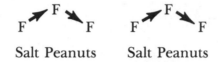

Salt Peanuts   Salt Peanuts

3. Do the same with resonator bells, which may be easier to work with since the letters on the notes eliminate the need to count up from the bottom A.

Happy Birthday Johann Strauss
(October 25)

Grades: 2-6.

Materials: Chalk and chalkboard; recording of *Die Fledermaus* by Johann Strauss; a cape; pictures of Batman and Robin; pictures of real bats; recording of *The Blue Danube* Waltz.

Concepts:

1. Any day might be the birthday of a famous composer.
2. Johann Strauss was known as the "Waltz King."
3. The waltz is a dance in 3/4 time or meter.

Activities
&
Directions

1. On the chalkboard, write:

HAPPY BIRTHDAY JOHANN STRAUSS
(October 25, 1825)

Ask your students to figure out how many years ago and in what country Johann Strauss was born. (He was born in Austria.) You might sing Happy Birthday as a waltz and even dance the waltz. As a background activity for listening to some of the waltzes from *Die Fledermaus* (The Bat), you might also find Austria on the map of Europe. It would be especially meaningful, before listening to *The Blue Danube* Waltz, for your students to find the river on the map and trace its route. To introduce a spirit of levity, try telling the children that "Strauss rhymes with mouse."

2. Other enjoyable activities center around the word *Fledermaus*, which means bat. This can be tied in with the spookiness of Halloween. The younger students can actually put on capes and act like bats, or at least like Batman. You can have a spine-chilling discussion of whether or not bats are scary, and if they attack humans or suck their blood!

3. *The Blue Danube* Waltz can also be discussed in relationship to its use in the movie *2001: A Space Odyssey*. Of course this depends on whether or not the youngsters have seen the film. An alternate activity is to teach the children how to waltz to this famous piece of music.

3

NOVEMBER

November is a month when most of the leaves have already fallen off the trees in the Northeast and when Jack Frost begins to appear. That nip in the air can be discouraging to adults, but to children it means they'll soon be able to make snowmen and snowballs. Soon they'll be able to use their sleds, skis, and ice skates.

November is a varied month. It starts out feeling like part of fall and ends up feeling more like winter. At the beginning of November we have Election Day. Toward the end of the month we have Thanksgiving. Almost smack in the middle of the month we have the patriotic Veterans Day. So, indeed, we have considerable variety.

Musically, too, there is much to choose from. Election Day songs that tell the history of this country are numerous and varied. Patriotic songs of our armed forces, or popular masterpieces such as "God Bless America," are also in plentiful supply. And who does not enjoy singing "Over the River and Through the Woods"? Who does not get aroused by the "Washington Post March" or "Stars and Stripes Forever"? Yes, November can be an exciting and musical month. Let's make it so! And enjoy it!

November

Figure 26

Grades: 2-7.

Materials: Chalk and chalkboard or music flashcards.

Concepts:

1. The musical staff, whole notes, half notes, quarter notes.
2. Highness and lowness of notes.
3. Music notes can have lines which go down on the left side or up on the right side. These lines are called *stems*.

**Activities
   &
Directions**

1. Place Figure 26 on the board or on music flash cards. Say to the children, "What letter does November begin with?" After getting the answer "N," ask the students to name songs, singers, musical instruments, or anything involved with music that begins with N. You might add National Music Camp (Interlochen, Michigan), NBC Radio, Natural (as opposed to sharp or flat), Neoclassicism, Neumes, or *Night on Bald Mountain* by Mussorgsky to those elicited from the students. Another enjoyable activity might be to listen to a *nocturne* by Chopin or *Nachtmusik (Eine Kleine Nachtmusik)* by Mozart. Many teachers have found nocturnes to be soothing and tranquilizing for use with young children.

2. By November your students should be able to identify musical Es, Bs, half notes, whole notes, and quarter notes. Use Figure 26 to quiz your children, asking them to name the musical notes between V and M in November. (Answer: E half notes.) Then ask them to tell you the musical notes between M and R in November. (Answer: B whole note and E quarter notes.) You might want to point out that the B is a whole note because

it is a circle that is not filled in and has no "stems" attached to it or that the first musical Es are half notes because they are whole notes with stems and the second musical E's are quarter notes because they are filled in and have stems. A good exercise that many music teachers have found successful is for the students to practice making whole, half, and quarter notes with the notes B and E. We've had great success using the words EBB, BE, and BEE to stress this concept.

3. Another good drill activity is to practice drawing high E's and low E's, high E's being "space notes" and low E's being "line notes" (see Figure 27). In this way the concept of highness and lowness can be demonstrated. After many high E's and low E's have been drawn as half notes, the children can color them in to change them to quarter notes. Incidentally, you might want to teach the concept of stems going up on the right side or down on the left side by telling your class that there are no small b's or q's when notes are made, only d's and p's.

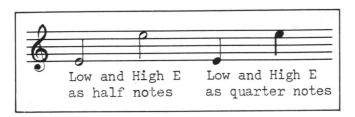

Low and High E
as half notes

Low and High E
as quarter notes

Figure 27

Election Day

Grades: 4-8.

Materials: Songs such as "I Like It Here," "This Is My Country," and "Give Me Your Tired, Your Poor"; recordings having to do with presidents or Election Day, such as those made by Oscar Brandt or Howard DaSilva (especially good songs are "Keep Cool and Keep Coolidge," "Wilson That's All," "If He's Good Enough for Lindy, He's Good Enough for Me," and "Row Row Row With Roosevelt."

Concepts:

1. The general election, always held the first Tuesday in November, gives registered voters the opportunity to vote for the candidate of their choice.

2. Political songs are a unique aspect of our American heritage and can be used to help us learn the history of our presidents (and our country).

**Activities
&
Directions**

1. It is important to discuss Election Day and its vital role in democracy. You can start by asking your students whom they would vote for and for whom their parents are voting. You might want to make a sample of an election ballot and have your class cast their votes. It might be fun to have as background music for this activity recordings about different elections and presidents such as those made by Oscar Brandt and Howard DaSilva. When playing a song such as "We Want Wilkie in the White House" (which uses the tune of "The Battle Hymn of the Republic") or "Do, Do, Do with Dewey," you might want to discuss the concept of alliteration. Or you can test your students' ability to name our presidents and then play "The Presidents" by Oscar Brandt, which uses the tune of "Yankee Doodle" to sing about all the presidents up to Eisenhower. You might want to explain that political songs are serious or humorous songs about something that happened in the political life of our country—and that there are many of them because of the freedom that we enjoy in the United States.

2. In the spirit of Election Day, it would be appropriate to sing patriotic songs, as many teachers have done throughout the years. You might want to try "I Like It Here," which uses *syncopation,* or displacement of the normal accents in music. Or you can sing the more familiar "Give Me Your Tired, Your Poor," which is based upon the words on the Statue of Liberty in New York Harbor, or the fairly simple "This Is My Country," which uses the "octave" we learned about in "Take Me Out to the Ballgame."

3. To reinforce note reading, Figure 28, which uses the musical notes A, C, D, and E, can be used. You can point out that Figure 28 contains eighth notes, which have connecting bars or flags as well as stems attached to notes that are filled in. You might retest students' knowledge of A, C, D, and E in music (see Figure 31, in which E and C are after EL and before TION).

Figure 28

School Days

Grades: 3-7.

Materials: Chalk and chalkboard or music flashcards.

Concepts:

1. 3/4 meter.
2. Dotted half notes.
3. Large skips (disjunct motion).

**Activities
&
Directions**

1. Place Figure 29 on the chalkboard or on music flashcards. You may want to have the children copy the music first, or you may want to sing the music first. Many music teachers have found that the symbols are more meaningful after the sound is demonstrated. Perhaps you can point to each dotted half note as you sing and then explain or review that a dotted half note is a circle with a stem that has a dot after it. Children can practice drawing dotted half notes. Or you can practice counting ONE two three, ONE two three, ONE two three, ONE two three as you point to the four dotted half notes. You may want to explain that 3/4 meter is called "waltz time," or you may call the

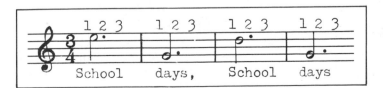

Figure 29

children's attention to the large skips between notes in these first four measures of the song "School Days." Practice may be needed in pointing to a dotted half note and giving it three counts. You can explain that the dot gives the note an extra count because the dot represents half of whatever the note is, a half note receiving two counts and the dot thus receiving one count. Finally, you can practice drawing and using the 3/4 conducting pattern with the students (see Figure 30) and then combining singing and conducting.

$\frac{3}{4}$ **conducting pattern**

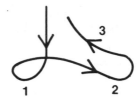

Figure 30

Montana Mood
(November 8)

Grades: K-8.

Materials: Cowboy or Western songs; toy cowboys, horses, wagons, and so on.

Concepts:

1. Montana is one of the states associated with the West, cowboys, and "cowboy songs."

2. Actually, most of the songs that we now think of as "cowboy songs" were written in the 1930's; for example, "Wagon Wheels," written by William J. "Billy" Hill.

**Activities
&
Directions**

1. Are there any children who have not seen hundreds of movies (between the movie theaters and television) where the cowboys are travelling from Texas, Wyoming, or the Dakotas to Montana? To celebrate the date (November 8, 1889) when Mon-

tana was admitted as a state, there are a number of possibilities. You and your class can listen to the "cowboy songs" that are associated with Roy Rogers and Gene Autrey movies, such as "Tumblin' Tumbleweed," "Wagon Wheels," and "Cool Water." You can talk about the "Wild West" and the many exciting sheriffs and outlaws. You can investigate books about how the West was won, even discussing the sensitive issue of our relationship with the American Indians.

2. With younger students, it might be fun to play "cowboys and Indians," "sheriffs and outlaws," or "good guys versus the bad guys." Cowboy songs (or country 'n' western music) can be played in the background. Many music teachers have found that second and third graders love to sing songs like "Cool Water" or, at least, join in with the opening lines: "All day I face the barren waste, without a drop of water, CO-OL WATER." (Often, the children with "spunk" will have fun with this song and howl like wolves, so don't become alarmed if they have even more fun than you planned!)

Puerto Rico Discovery Month

Grades: 2-8.

Materials: Latin percussion instruments, such as *congas claves, guiros, maracas, timbales,* and *bongos.*

Concepts:

1. Many of our exciting dances, while not necessarily originating in Puerto Rico, came to the United States via Puerto Rican Americans. Some of these are the *merengue, cha-cha, mambo,* and the more recent *salza* or *salsa.*

2. Many of the instruments used in modern jazz or dance orchestras, while not necessarily originating in Puerto Rico, came to this country or gained popularity through Puerto Rican jazz and dance orchestras.

Activities & Directions

1. On the chalkboard, write:
   NOVEMBER: PUERTO RICO DISCOVERY MONTH
   (November 19, 1493)

and discuss the status of Puerto Rico. You might explain, for example, that Puerto Rico is not a state and there is considerable controversy in Puerto Rico over whether the tiny island should seek independance or statehood. You can tie-in with map studies and social studies by locating the island or, in the lower grades, explaining what an island is and how it differs from a peninsula. With older students you might discuss how we obtained Puerto Rico from Spain in the Spanish American War, which is why Puerto Ricans speak Spanish.

2. We've had fun with games that we have named "Bang the Bongos" or "Catch the Conga." Of course, it is necessary to have the instruments. In "Catch the Conga," a student carrying a conga runs past a line of children who try to strike the instrument. The "winner" is the student who succeeds in striking the *conga* and getting a fairly decent sound. "Bang the Bongos" also involves trying to obtain a good sound or tone. The bongos are held between the legs and struck with the tips of one's fingers. There are many recordings available that feature the sound of *bongos,* and it might be advisable to play one for the children to have them hear what the proper tone sounds like. For the sound of the *conga,* any recording by Mongo Santamaria can be used.

3. Popular dances that came from Puerto Rico or through Puerto Rico can also be used to celebrate Puerto Rico Discovery Month. Even the *hustle* has a Latin flavor, and there are specific steps called the *Latin Hustle. Mambos, cha-chas,* and *merengues* can also be used. If you can, you can demonstrate the steps for your children. Even for listening, many of these dances are quite exciting. They can be used as background music, while your students investigate books about Puerto Rican foods, customs, and other aspects of the culture.

Veterans Day

Grades: K-6.

Materials: Recordings of John Philip Sousa marches, such as "Stars and Stripes Forever," "El Capitan," and "Washington Post March"; recording of Vladimer Horowitz playing "Stars and Stripes Forever"; words and music for patriotic songs such as "The Marine's Hymn," "When the Caissons Go Rolling Along," and "Off We Go Into the Wild Blue Yonder."

Concepts:

1. On Veterans Day men and women parade in uniforms that represent their branch of the Armed Forces: land, sea, or air.

2. On Veterans Day we can hear many marching bands. Marches use 2/4, 4/4, or 6/8 meters.

Activities
&
Directions

1. Younger children enjoy marching or dressing up like soldiers and sailors. You might prepare for this lesson by asking your students to come to school with at least part of a uniform from some branch of the service or with toy planes, boats, jeeps, and so on. Then, on the day of the lesson, you can stage your own parade. Some children will be in the army, some in the navy, some in the marines, and some in the air force. As they march around the room they can say ONE two, ONE two or ONE two three four, ONE two three four, thus developing a concept of 2/4 and 6/8 meter, in which there are two beats to a measure, and 4/4 meter, in which there are four beats to a measure. As background music for the parade, you can play familiar marches by John Philip Sousa, sometimes known as the "March King" of America. See if you and your students can discover where the heavy accents fall to determine whether there are two or four beats to the measure.

2. Another enjoyable activity is to sing songs such as the well-known "Marine's Hymn." You might want to discuss its background. The "Marine's Hymn" was written in 1847 when the United States was at war with Mexico. The tune came from an old French opera. Map studies can be used in conjunction with this lesson. The children can locate Mexico on the map, and you can relate this to the first line of the song "From the Halls of Montezuma" by explaining that Montezuma was the King of the Aztecs when Mexico was conquered by Cortez.

3. For older students, you might want to compare a recording of a marching band playing "Stars and Stripes Forever" with one by the piano virtuoso Vladimer Horowitz, in which he plays his

own variations on this march. You can do the same thing with younger students, but include more activity, such as the children making believe they are playing the piano as the Horowitz recording is being played. We've had success with this type of an approach, and the children love to act out being a virtuoso at the piano—even the stage entrance and sitting down at the piano bench.

Pentatonic Play

Grades: 3-8.

Materials: School piano, portable organ, toy piano, pianica (which has an accordian keyboard but is played by blowing into it, sometimes called a melodica), or an accordian if one is available.

Concepts:

1. One of the ways of playing a pentatonic or five note scale is by playing the black keys of the piano, organ, pianica, or accordian.
2. Black keys are the sharps (♯) or flats (♭) of a scale. (Note to the teacher: sometimes white keys function as sharps or flats.)

**Activities
     &
Directions**

1. This lesson can also be a follow-up to a lesson such as "What's New on Television?" First, ask your students to bring in toy pianos, accordians, or melodicas. When they have been brought to school, or you have a piano in the room, have the children explore the black keys. Explain that one way of playing a pentatonic or five note scale is by playing only the black keys. Explain also that the black keys are sharps or flats of the scale, drawing a sharp (♯) and a flat (♭) on the chalkboard. Now, ask the children if they can come up with any familiar songs, radio or television themes, or tunes from commercials. If none are discovered, we suggest that they try to play "Mary Had a Little Lamb," "Old MacDonald," or "Auld Lang Syne" (see Figure 31).

Figure 31

2. Another enjoyable activity is to place two fingers of the left hand on the two black keys (C♯ and D♯) and three fingers of the right hand on three black keys (F♯, G♯, and A♯). Then, using this position, try to discover tunes by using different combinations of the two and three fingers. Below are some we have found can be used successfully. (Note: remember that the right hand is 3,4,5 *not* 1,2,3.

ARE YOU SLEEPING

    3 4 5 3   3 4 5 3

ROW, ROW, ROW YOUR BOAT

    3 3   3 4 5

NOBODY KNOWS THE TROUBLE I'VE SEEN

    5 1 2 3   4 5 5 5 5

AULD LANG SYNE

    1 3 3 3 5   4 3 4 5 4 3 . . . .

THREE BLIND MICE

    5 4 3   5 4 3

3. Some children love to play the black keys in order, one at a time, such as 1 2 3 4 5 4 3 2 1, 1 2 3 4, 5 4 3 2, 1 2 3 4, 5 4 3 2, and so on. This gives a "bluesy" feel, which is very stimulating and which many teachers have found to be successful. Finally, playing two black keys at a time can sound like American Indian music if the two notes are far enough apart, such as G♯ and D♯, or F♯ and C♯.

Robert Fulton's Birthday
(November 14)

Grades: 2-6.

Materials: Recording or music for the song "Erie Canal"; toy steamboats or toy boats representing steamboats.

Concepts:

1. The song "Erie Canal" is an American folksong about the canal between the Hudson River and Lake Erie.

2. A canal is a man-made body of water that connects the sea to a lake or connects two oceans. The Erie Canal connects Lake Erie to the Atlantic Ocean by way of the Hudson River.

**Activities
&
Directions**

1. As background for this lesson, you might provide some details about Robert Fulton, whom some claim invented the steamboat. (Originally an artist, he became an engineer and won prominence as an expert on canals.) At any rate, he was the first to obtain a patent for the steamboat. Related activities can involve finding the Erie Canal and Lake Erie on the map, discussing the basic principle of how the steam engine works, and listening to the folk song "Erie Canal."

2. After writing on the chalkboard

    HAPPY BIRTHDAY ROBERT FULTON
    (November 14, 1765)

    you might ask your students what happened 100 years after he was born. (Answer: the Civil War ended.) You might even ask the younger children, "How many days after Election Day was he born?" or "How many days after what is now Veterans Day was he born?" Some students find questions such as these a lot of fun.

3. A little game that some children find enjoyable can result in their never forgetting where F in the treble clef is. It involves their placing toy steamboats, or toy boats representing steamboats, on the staff in the first space F (for Fulton) or top line F (for Fulton). (See Figure 32.)

steamboats
on the
staff

Figure 32

Oklahoma
(November 16)

Grades: 3-8.

Materials: Recording of the full score or excerpts of the Rogers and Hammerstein musical *Oklahoma;* cowboy and farmer outfits or pitchforks; a very large trunk.

Concepts:

1. Broadway musicals are among America's unique contributions to music.
2. For close to two decades, the team of Richard Rogers and Oscar Hammerstein wrote broadway musicals that achieved worldwide recognition and acclaim. (Rogers wrote the music, and Hammerstein wrote the lyrics.) Among the best known of their works are *Carousel, The King and I, South Pacific,* and *Oklahoma.*

**Activities
&
Directions**

1. On the chalkboard, write:

OKLAHOMA GRANTED STATEHOOD
(November 16, 1907)

Ask the students to compute how many years ago this was as a mathematical excercise. On a map of the United States they can locate the state of Oklahoma. You might use an atlas to obtain background information on crops, terrain, and climate. This will tie-in nicely with work in social studies. Then go back to the date and ask questions such as "Who was the president at this time?" and "How many years before we entered the first world war was Oklahoma admitted as a state?"

2. The story of *Oklahoma* is an interesting one involving the traditional feud between cowboys and farmers, a "girl who can't say no," a "surrey with a fringe on top," and the typical "wind sweeping down the plains." You might also use some of the lyrics from the song "Oh What a Beautiful Morning" to allude to the corn being ". . . as high as an elephant's eye." The record jacket can be used to obtain more details about the plot. The story is similar to Romeo and Juliet, with the youngsters being worried that "People will say we're in love" and the complication of feuding farmers and cowboys preventing this.

3. A particularly fun activity, especially for third and fourth grade children, is for them to dress up like cowboys and farmers. You can then play "The Farmers and the Cowboys Will Be Friends" from *Oklahoma,* which has a lively, lilting, polka-like rhythm. The children can clap their hands in rhythm, as is done at a hoedown, do a polka or a square dance, or yell "yahoo" whenever they get the urge. Many music teachers have found that this song has a great deal of musical excitement and is quite effective.

4. Another "skit" that works well involves the *Oklahoma* song "Poor Jud Is Dead." You can drape a large trunk in black to make it look like a coffin. Then you can have a mock funeral as this song is played in the background. Actually, in the musical, the song is a satirical number or "spoof" (and this comes through in the song, making the whole thing amusing rather than sad).

5. Finally, you might want to use the title song, making it more commemorative of the day Oklahoma was granted statehood.

Figure 33

You will probably find that your students will particularly enjoy that passage in which they spell out "O K L A H O M A, Oklahoma, O.K." Try having your class strike their palms with a fist as they say, rhythmically, O K L A H O M A (see Figure 33).

Carolina in the Morning
(November 21)

Grades: 3-8.

Materials: Recording of the song "Nothing Could Be Finer Than to Be in Carolina in the Morning."

Concepts:

1. Repetition of a melodic figure.
2. *Sequence* is the process of repeating a melodic figure at a step above or below the note on which the figure started.

**Activities
&
Directions**

1. On the chalkboard, place Figure 34.

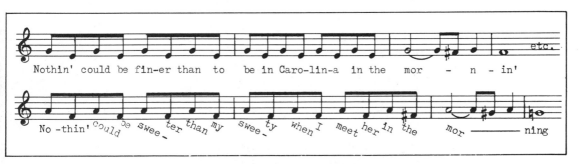

Figure 34

2. Point out that the first phrase starts on G and the second phrase starts on A. Explain that the second phrase starts higher than the first and that this repetition a note higher is called *sequence* in music. After listening to a recording of the song, you might try singing these two phrases, pointing to the notes on the chalkboard as you sing.

Opening of Guys and Dolls
(November 24)

Grades: 4-8.

Materials: Recording of *Guys and Dolls* or just the "Fugue" (more popularly known as "I Got the Horse Right Here"; racing forms or "scratch sheets."

Concepts:

1. A fugue in music is similar to a round, or canon, in that musical "imitation" is used.
2. Broadway musicals are among America's unique contributions to the music of the world.

Activities
&
Directions

1. Place on the chalkboard:

    OPENING OF *GUYS AND DOLLS*
    (November 24, 1950)

    As preparation for this lesson, you might compute how long ago this was or discuss the music of the 1950's (such as Elvis Presley or other rock 'n' roll or rhythm 'n' blues stars). With older students you might want to discuss the Korean War and the presidencies of Harry S. Truman and Dwight D. Eisenhower.

2. One activity that we've had great success with is as follows. It involves the boys and girls dressing up like gamblers and gun molls, using black shirts and white ties and simple props such as racing forms. Play the fugue from *Guys and Dolls,* which starts off "I got the horse right here, his name is Paul Revere. . . ." Children love this little skit, and you should also!

Thanksgiving

Grades: K-8.

Materials: Recordings of *Harvest Home Chorale* by Charles Ives, *Plow That Broke the Plains* by Virgil Thompson, "Pilgrims' Chorus" from the opera *Tannhauser* by Richard Wagner; recordings or music for the song "Come Ye Thankful People Come" by Malcolm Williamson and the Navaho Indian "Corn Grinding Song."

Concepts:

1. In the United States, we celebrate Thanksgiving on the last Thursday in November.

2. Thanksgiving always takes place after the harvest season. The first Thanksgiving celebration was observed by American Indians and Pilgrims to America eating together in peace.

3. Richard Wagner's opera *Tannhauser* contains a "Pilgrims' Chorus."

Activities
&
Directions

1. As background for this lesson, you might want to use a map and have children find Plymouth Rock, where the Pilgrims landed in America. Or you can capitalize on the love that many third and fourth graders have for dressing up like Pilgrims or Indians. Background music for these activities can be *Plow That Broke the Plains* or *Harvest Home Chorale*. (Perhaps you can tell the children that a "chorale" is a hymn tune sung in the Protestant church of Germany during the second half of the 16th century. Explain that the chorales of Charles Ives are different in sound from the more traditional chorales because they were composed hundreds of years later.) You might remember, also, that many city children are not acquainted with an old fashioned plow. Find a picture of one and take it to class so that they can see that farmers did not have the conveniences shown on some commercials on television.

2. Many music teachers have found that the "Corn Grinding Song" provides a good basis for a Thanksgiving musical activity. You can find descriptions of how corn grinding takes place and share this information with the students. Also, you can have students make a list of foods that come from corn. You can also discuss some of the crops Indians had when European settlers came to the new world. A humorous approach is to

mention Mazola Margerine and how the name is taken from the Indian name for corn—*maze*.

3. Discussion can also center around the whole concept of the harvest season and how important the harvest season is to all countries. You might want to discuss the different lengths of harvest seasons. The harvest season is longer in the South and Southwest and shorter in the North, the shorter harvest season making it all the more crucial that the harvest be an abundant one. For younger students, explain the meaning of harvesting crops in greater detail. With this in mind, the *Harvest Home Chorale* might have greater meaning, as would singing the familiar "Come Ye Thankful People Come." You might ask your students if they know any prayers regarding the harvest, such as "Prayer of Thanksgiving." Ask if any boy or girl can sing part of "Now Thank We All Our God." It might be appropriate to explain that some of the songs we sing for Thanksgiving actually came from different countries and were used for different purposes. For example, "Prayer of Thanksgiving" came from the Netherlands and was used to celebrate the liberation of the Netherlands from Spain.

4. In the upper grades, you can discuss the relationship of Indians and Pilgrims celebrating the harvest in peace and the Netherlands celebrating their liberation from Spanish domination—how both are "thankful" and giving thanks through prayer. We have also had success in the upper grades with "Pilgrims' Chorus" from the opera *Tannhauser* by Wagner (pronounced *Vahgner*). You might ask the students if the "Pilgrims' Chorus" sounds like a prayer or if they think Wagner necessarily meant the American Pilgrims? Related map activities can be finding Spain, Germany, and the Netherlands on the map of Europe.

Staffs of Corn

Grades: 2-4.

Materials: Chalk and chalkboard or music flash cards.

Concepts:

1. Learning music notes can be fun.
2. Homonymns.

**Activities
&
Directions**

1. Place Figure 35 on the chalkboard or music flashcards.

2. Humorously ask the children if an "ear" of corn is the same kind of "ear" you hear with. Explain that homonymns are words that sound alike but mean different things; thus, an ear of corn is an expression used for one of the corns on a "stalk" (another homonymn?). Refer to Figure 35 and show how we can have fun by using corn on a staff instead of musical notes. Show how we are using the corns to spell F A C E (and you might want to joke about using "ears" to spell face). This is a very enjoyable "fun activity," and we've had great success with it. Try it.

staffs
of
corn
(musical ears)

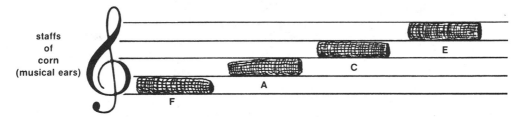

Figure 35

Pumpkin Pie

Grades: K-4.

Materials: A pumpkin pie; chalk and chalkboard.

Concepts:

1. Music notes in America get their rhythmic values from the concept of fractions.

2. A pie can be used to explain the concept behind whole, half, quarter, eighth, and sixteenth notes.

**Activities
&
Directions**

1. Place Figure 36 on the chalkboard. Explain how a circle can be divided into halves, quarters, eighths, and sixteenths. Do it

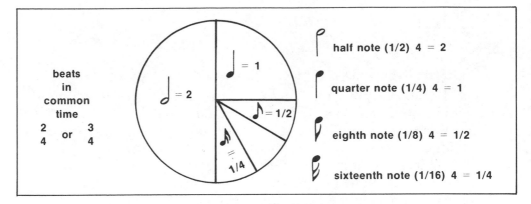

Figure 36

several times, showing the circle becoming two parts, then four parts, then eight parts, and finally sixteen parts. Explain that music is the same way. There are half notes, quarter notes, and so on. For the older children, you might want to discuss counting and beats. Explain that in "common time," or 4/4 meter, the whole note represents four beats, the half note represents half of four, or two, and so forth (see Figure 36).

2. It might be more fun, and certainly tastier, to use a pumpkin pie to demonstrate dividing a circle into halves, quarters, eighths, and sixteenths. Then, after the exercise is over, you can eat the pie. (You might have to exercise after this exercise!)

Telephone Tapes

Grades: 4-8.

Materials: Cassette tape recorders and blank cartridges.

Concepts:

1. Creativity does not have to be beyond the reach of the average child.
2. Children can create their own compositions using some basic electronic sounds.

**Activities
&
Directions**

1. Here is a fun activity that can be used to help forestall the "winter doldrums." Ask your students if they have tape recorders at home. If available, you can lend some school tape recorders to your children. Tell them that you want them to record the "busy signals" and "push button noises" that the telephone makes and call these sounds *section A*. Then they are to record the sounds the telephone makes when it is left off the hook and call these sounds *section B*. Play some of these "compositions" in class, both consecutively and simultaneously. Ask your children if they had fun making them and listening to each other's compositions.

2. Another way of using the children's "telephone tapes" is to compare them with recorded electronic music. You might ask the children for their ideas about the similarities and differences among their own little creative endeavors and the work of professionals. If you did the lesson entitled 4′ 33″, ask your children if they see any similarities between John Cage's type of experimentalism and this type of an experiment. We have found that this can lead to several days' worth of discussions about traditional versus experimental music.

COMPOSERS OF THE MONTH

Happy Birthday W. C. Handy

Grades: 5-8.

Materials: Chalk and chalkboard; record player; recording of W. C. Handy's music (preferably one that contains *St. Louis Blues).*

Concepts:

1. W. C. Handy was a black American musician who is well known for songs that he composed.

2. Some songs that W. C. Handy composed were in "the blues form." Sometimes Handy is called the "Father of the blues."

3. Along with jazz, "the blues form" is among black America's outstanding contributions to music.

Activities
&
Directions

1. After explaining that in the South many blacks were not given birth certificates (and thus didn't know their exact birthdays), write on the board:

HAPPY BIRTHDAY W. C. HANDY

November 1873

When you sing "Happy Birthday" to Handy, you might first sing it "straight" and then try to jazz it up or give it a "blues" feeling. A recording of W. C. Handy's music can be played in order to get a feeling for the way certain tones are "bent" or sung a little "flat." The numbers one through seven can be placed on the board, with flats over the third and seventh steps to show which tones are usually flattened: 1, 2, (♭)3, 4, 5, 6, (♭)7. Then try singing "Happy Birthday" with a blues feeling again.

2. You can almost insure a successful lesson if one of your students plays the guitar. Explaining that "the blues" is both a style of music and a specific harmonic form (there are specific types of chord changes that are used), ask if anyone can explain what a chord is. Write C E G on the board and have your guitarist play it separately and simultaneously, defining a chord as three or more tones played simultaneously, often with a harmonious sound. (See Figure 37.)

Sample blues harmonic form or chord progression.

Figure 37

Happy Birthday John Philip Sousa
(November 6)

Grades: K-8.

Materials: Any marches by John Philip Sousa.

Concepts:

1. John Philip Sousa was known as the March King of America.
2. The sousaphone, a musical instrument, was named after John Philip Sousa.

**Activities
&
Directions**

1. Place on the chalkboard:

   HAPPY BIRTHDAY JOHN PHILIP SOUSA
   (November 6, 1854)

   Discuss the coincidence that John Philip Sousa's birthday is in November, the same month as *Veterans Day.* Isn't it interesting, you might ask, that the man best known for military marches such as "Stars and Stripes Forever" should be born five days before the day on which we honor the men who served this country in times of war?

2. Another enjoyable activity is to sing "Happy Birthday" as a march. Younger students can even stand up and march around the room as they sing. You might want to try playing the very beginning of a Sousa march and then lift the needle and begin to sing "Happy Birthday." This can be very successful and a lot of fun to try. (We hope it works!) You can also turn down the volume instead of lifting the needle so that there is a trace of a beat to follow.

3. Pictures of the sousaphone can be shown to students who have never seen one. If a film or filmstrip that shows a marching band is available, the sousaphone can be seen in action. To isolate the sound of the sousaphone, tuba music can be used, because the sousaphone is a type of tuba. You might even use *Tubby the Tuba.*

Happy Birthday Aaron Copland
(November 14)

Grades: 2-8.

Materials: Recordings of *El Salon Mexico, Appalachian Spring,* and *Billy the Kid* by Aaron Copland; Mexican sombreros or cowboy hats; toy cowboys and horses for second, third, and fourth graders.

Concepts:

　　1. Aaron Copland was born in Brooklyn, New York.

　　2. Copland used "folk songs" or traditional melodies in many of his compositions—making some of his earlier compositions "Nationalistic" in style.

Activities
&
Directions

　　1. On the chalkboard, write:

HAPPY BIRTHDAY AARON COPLAND
(November 14, 1900)

Ask your students to figure out how many years ago Aaron Copland was born. Many music teachers have focused on the fact that Aaron Copland was born at the very beginning of the century, in 1900. When you sing "Happy Birthday" to Aaron Copland, it might be fun to think of Billy the Kid (about whom one of Copland's most famous compositions was written) riding on his horse. You can then try to sing "Happy Birthday" in cowboy style. (Note: the children in lower grades will love to bob up and down while singing, as though they were on horses.) You might even draw an analogy between Aaron Copland and Billy the Kid both being born in New York.

　　2. Preparation and background for listening to *El Salon Mexico* can center around finding Mexico on a map or reviewing the history of Mexico and how the Aztecs were cruelly conquered. Similarly, as preparation for listening to *Billy the Kid,* you might discuss the Wild West, finding on a map the area of our country that was considered the Wild West for many years.

3. Another enjoyable activity is to do the Mexican Hat Dance. This is excellent preparation for *El Salon Mexico,* and children love this activity! Sombreros can be worn or danced around. You might even discuss the bullfights in Mexico. Then play some of *El Salon Mexico* and ask the children if they find the music exciting. We hope they will, and you can explain that some of the musical excitement is created by changing, or variable, meter—switching from 6/8 to 3/4 time, as shown in Figure 38. You might develop a "feel" for changing, or variable, meter by having the students count: ONE two three FOUR five six/ ONE two THREE four FIVE six. Explain that meter is created by accents falling on certain beats.

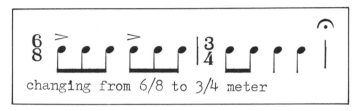

changing from 6/8 to 3/4 meter

Figure 38

4. You might mention the fact that Aaron Copland traveled to France to study with the famous Nadia Boulanger (pronounced Bou-lahn-jay), who taught many of the most famous composers in the world. A map might be used with younger students, who might not be sure where France is.

5. It is fun to listen to *Billy the Kid* and try to name the several traditional melodies or "folk songs" that are used. You might listen informally several times and have your children raise their hands when they think they hear a folk song. Or you can ask them to list the American folk songs used in their notebooks. Among the ones you should finally identify are:
   (1) "I Ride an Old Paint"
   (2) "Great Grand Dad"
   (3) "The Dying Cowboy"

4

DECEMBER

In most parts of this country and, indeed, in many parts of the world, there is no happier month for children than December. Pleasant thoughts of Christmas fill their minds. Also, and perhaps quite naturally, the expectation of snow, sleds, skis, and ice skates also enters children's minds. Why not capitalize on all of this fun? Just the thought of singing "Jingle Bells" and "I'm Dreaming of a White Christmas" is usually enough to change any frown to a smile.

Musical birthdays abound in December. We have chosen to include those of Sibelius, Beethoven, Deems Taylor, and Puccini. There are musical ways of celebrating French Conversation Week, and there are many fun-filled ways of commemorating the dates in December on which Mississippi, Indiana, Pennsylvania, and Alabama were admitted to the Union as states. Thus, this almanack continues to blend a chronological and a musical approach to make each month, week, and day alive with musical excitement.

Enjoy a jolly December!

December

Figure 39

Grades: 2-7.

Materials: Chalk and chalkboard or music flashcards.

Concepts

1. Each letter of the alphabet can open up a world of music.
2. The musical alphabet is A through G. When a treble clef is present, the space between the middle line and the next-to-the-bottom line is "A." As you go forward in the alphabet, you go *up* in music.
3. There are five lines to the musical *staff*.

**Activities
&
Directions**

1. Place Figure 39 on the board or on music flashcards. If you have used similar lessons in September, October, and November, your students should be well acquainted with the staff and what the notes are. If not, this lesson is purposely simplified. The notes representing the first four letters in DECEMBER (DECE) are all whole notes, and the musical alphabet (A B C D E F G) is written on the staff (see Figure 39). You might start by counting the five lines of the staff, reciting the musical alphabet (A B C D E F G), or pointing to A B C D E F G on the staff in the diagram. It might be amusing, on the other hand, to see the humor in Figure 39 and see the "words" *Mo, Moo,* and *Rabcdefg* in the figure! Try asking your students if these nonsense words will enable them to remember the musical alphabet.
2. Say to the children, "What letter does December begin with?"

After getting the answer "D," ask the students to name songs, singers, musical instruments, or anything involved with music that begins with D. You might add drums, Delius, Debussy, and Dvorak (or any others that you might think of) to those elicited from the students. This activity is usually fun! Try it!

Using Popular Music and the Radio in Class

Grades: 2-8.

Materials: School radio or student transistor radios.

Concepts:

1. There are many different styles of music.
2. Different radio stations play different styles and cater to different tastes.

**Activities
&
Directions**

1. There is nothing that makes children happier than having their teacher show acceptance of what they like. One way of doing this is by accepting the radio stations your children listen to. Prepare for this exciting lesson by telling your students that they can bring radios to school and will be permitted to turn to their favorite station. On the day of the lesson, call upon several children to individually turn to their favorite ones and then to identify the song, the recording group, and the style of the music being played. Begin listing the styles—or dances—on the chalkboard. Try to elicit descriptions such as popular music, rock, soul, jazz, and Latin.

2. Another effective way of using the radio is as follows. Ask your students if they—or their parents, older brothers, and sisters—ever listen to classical music at home. For students who may be unfamiliar with the sound of classical music, play a classical station so that they can hear its sound. Then play a game of turning the dial, stopping on different stations, and trying to identify the style of the music. At certain points you may find students raising their hands to tell you: "That's the kind of music my father listens to!" At those times, you can identify what kind of music it is. Perhaps you'll be able to go

more deeply into just what factors make up style: beats, sound, the length, the instruments used. It will be helpful if you can list any important conclusions on the board.

Chicago, Chicago. . . .
(December 3)

Grades: 3-8.

Materials: Recordings of songs such as "My Kind of Town, Chicago Is" or the score to the Broadway musical *Chicago*; pictures of Chicago (the "windy city").

Concepts:

1. Chicago is one of the largest cities in the United States.
2. Both songs and a Broadway musical have been inspired by the "windy city," Chicago.

**Activities
&
Directions**

1. Write on the chalkboard:

    ILLINOIS ADMITTED TO THE UNION
    December 3, 1818

2. If you're a fan of Frank Sinatra, you're probably familiar with his recordings of both "best known" songs about Chicago: "My Kind of Town, Chicago Is" and "Chicago, Chicago, a Wonderful Town." Such songs can be used to kick-off this lesson. Or you might show pictures of the "windy city," as it is often called, and have your students make believe they are fighting the wind while walking up a steep hill. This can be fun! Using a map to locate first Illinois and then Chicago would be more formal, but it might be necessary to get a general idea of their locations. Illinois is one of our nation's many Indian names, and you might want to compare it with Iroquois, the Indian tribe, showing letter changes and how similar they are in spelling.

3. The broadway musical *Chicago* can be used for discussing and comparing New York and Chicago. Their differences and similarities regarding size, products manufactured, tourist at-

tractions, and so on, can be discussed. Perhaps you can use almanacs and an atlas to obtain more specific details. At any rate, the musical score for *Chicago* is exciting, and many music teachers have had good results with it. You should enjoy the music. It's worth a try.

French Conversation Week
(First Week in December)

Grades: 3-8.

Materials: Chalk and chalkboard; recording of the French national anthem; recordings of other French songs and "Dites-moi" from *South Pacific*.

Concepts:

1. The United States and France have had a long friendship, ever since the American Revolution.
2. "Frere Jacques," a song known by most American school children, is a "round."
3. Tchaikovsky used the French national anthem in his famous *1812 Overture*.

**Activities
&
Directions**

1. On the chalkboard, write:

FRENCH CONVERSATION WEEK
(First Week in December)

You might be lucky enough to have a French language program in your school, so that some of your students speak or are learning French. In this case, it will probably be easy to get students to locate France and its capital, Paris, on the map of Europe. It might even be easy to get some of the students to sing French songs taught to them by their French teacher. If not, you might want to try singing the familiar "Frere Jacques," explaining that this song is a *round,* in which there is both musical *imitation* and different sections that harmonize with each other. Many music teachers have found that children enjoy the song "Dites-moi" from the Broadway musical *South*

Pacific because it is sung by children in the musical and on the recordings.

"Dites-moi" from *South Pacific*

Dites-moi, pourquoi, la vie est belle
Dites-moi, pourquoi, la vie est gai
Dites-moi, pourquoi, chere mademoiselle,
Est-ce-que, parce que, vous m'aimez

2. Another enjoyable activity is to listen to the exciting *1812 Overture* by Tchaikovsky. Children enjoy both the story of Napoleon's army being defeated by the Russian winter as well as army and the sound of the real canons that are used on many recordings. We've had success with this lesson and hope you will too!

Mississippi
(December 10)

Grades: 3-8.

Materials: Chalk and chalkboard; map of the United States; recording of Ferde Grofe's *Mississppi Suite*.

Concept: Ferde Grofe, the famous composer of the *Grand Canyon Suite*, also wrote a *Mississippi Suite*.

Activities
&
Directions

1. Place on the chalkboard:

MISSISSIPPI GRANTED STATEHOOD
December 10, 1817

See if your students can figure out that this was exactly one century before the United States entered the first World War. As background for this lesson, you might discuss the Louisiana Purchase and how we acquired the land from Napoleon when he needed money. Mississippi can be located on the map, and you can have lots of fun asking your class to spell Mississippi. Younger children, in particular, love all the s's and i's. The

Mississippi River can be traced and compared in size with the Nile and Amazon rivers.

2. You can now play part of *Mississippi Suite* by Ferde Grofe, asking your students if they have ever heard the more famous *Grand Canyon Suite* by the same composer. Does the music describe a powerful river as well as one part of the *Grand Canyon Suite* describes a desert? Listen and find out! Some teachers who use the *Mississippi Suite* use *Huckleberry Finn* as a "motivation," many children knowing this delightful book about life on the Mississippi. As the music is played, younger children, in particular, might like to re-enact the famous scene of Jim and Huckleberry Finn on a raft.

Back Home in Indiana
(December 11)

Grades: 2-8.

Materials: Chalk and chalkboard; railroad hat or uniform; recordings of "Back Home in Indiana" and "Wabash Cannonball"; pictures of trains or toy or miniature trains.

Concept: The beginning of the song "Back Home in Indiana" uses four notes that are a type of "bugle call" or part of the *overtone series*. (See Figure 40.)

Figure 40

Activities
&
Directions

1. Write on the chalkboard:

INDIANA ADMITTED TO THE UNION
December 11, 1816

2. Background for this lesson can be provided by finding Indiana

and the Wabash River on the map. Historically, 1816 can be seen as much closer to the War of 1812 than to the Civil War. Art skills can be drawn upon by some students drawing the state of Indiana or tracing it, as many children love to do.

3. So many children love to dress up in all types of costumes. One of the "get-ups" that many children love is that of a train engineer—one reason that Casey Jones is such a popular folk hero. If one of your students has a conductor's cap or a full train engineer's uniform, you can "play" at being a train engineer. This might tie in nicely with the song "Wabash Cannonball," and you and your students can determine whether this was a real or imaginery train.

4. If you don't want to chance being unable to determine whether the "Wabash Cannonball" ever really streaked across the plains of Indiana near the Wabash River, you can use the more accessible "Back Home in Indiana," whose opening four notes are like a bugle call or the second, third, fourth, and fifth overtones of the *overtone series* (see Figure 40). This is a fun song that can be found on many Dixieland Jazz recordings.

A Few Bars—Maestro Please
(December 12)

Grades: K-5.

Materials: Chalk and chalkboard; recording of "The Pennsylvania Polka"; small Hershey chocolate bars.

Concepts:

1. Pennsylvania was founded by William Penn and the Quakers, who were seeking religious freedom.
2. Philadelphia is the home of the Liberty Bell.
3. There are both "bars" of music and "bars" of candy; the word has two meanings.

**Activities
&
Directions**

1. With young children, there is nothing that motivates interest faster than the taste buds! This lesson will be a success the

moment your children see a pile of Hershey candy bars. By the way, the only reason we specify Hershey bars is that they come from Hershey, Pennsylvania. You might want to have one of your more dramatic students say "A FEW BARS—MAESTRO PLEASE" and be rewarded with Hershey candy bars instead of a few bars of music. Or you can respond to the request for a few bars by simultaneously both giving out candy and playing some of The Pennsylvania Polka, to which the students and you can dance. Then go on to explain that Pennsylvania, one of the original states, was admitted to the union on December 12. Doesn't this sound like fun?

2. With older students, you might start out in a more serious way, placing on the chalkboard:

> "PROCLAIM LIBERTY AND JUSTICE
> THROUGHOUT ALL THE LAND
> AND UNTO ALL THE INHABITANTS THEREOF."

Before playing a rollicking polka as a treat, discussion can center around William Penn and the Quakers (who were in quest of religious freedom) founding Pennsylvania. See if your students can discover where the above words appear. (Answer: the Liberty Bell). You might even ring bells, to represent the Liberty Bell; bells are musical instruments, too!

With My Banjo on My Knee
(December 14)

Grades: 2-8.

Materials: Chalk and chalkboard; recordings of the songs "Oh! Susannah," and "Stars Fell on Alabama"; pictures of a banjo or a banjo itself.

Concepts:

1. Alabama was not one of the original 13 states but was admitted to the Union soon after the American Revolution.
2. "Oh! Susannah!" is a song by Stephen Foster.
3. The banjo is a string instrument that is both strummed and plucked (or "picked"). It is often used alongside a guitar in folk, bluegrass, or country and western music.

**Activities
&
Directions**

1. "Oh! Susannah!" is a song by Stephen Foster that has been used for many years by teachers, with great success. It can serve as an excellent motivation for interest in the date of Alabama's entry into the United States of America. The words are easily available in many songbooks, and children love the visual image of "I come from Alabama with my banjo on my knee." Perhaps you might want to use a discovery approach instead. After placing on the chalkboard:

   ALABAMA ADMITTED AS A STATE
   December 14, 1819

   you might ask your students if they know of any songs that mention Alabama. They might come up with "Oh! Susannah!" or "Stars Fell on Alabama." Either song can then be played; both are enjoyable. If "Oh! Susannah!" is chosen, you can get into a discussion of the banjo, showing pictures of it or having someone demonstrate the real thing. You might even compare styles of music that use both the banjo and guitar, such as folk, bluegrass, or country and western.

2. The song "Oh! Susannah!" might be used for motivating a more serious discussion about Alabama. Alabama figures prominently in the history of black America. Alabama is the home of one of the more prestigious centers of learning, which for many years was a totally segregated college, the Tuskegee Institute, founded in 1881 by Booker T. Washington. You might even discuss the fact that Montgomery, Alabama, was the scene of the late 1950's bus boycott, which was started by Rosa Park but led by the late Dr. Martin Luther King, Jr.

3. If interest in the banjo is aroused when the song "Oh! Susannah!" is sung, played, or discussed, you might want to play a very popular banjo recording from a few years back that made the hit parade. It was called "Dueling Banjos" and might still be easily available.

Boston Tea Party Anniversary
(December 16)

Grades: 2-8.

Materials: Any patriotic songs or American Indian dress.

Concept: The anniversary of the Boston Tea Party is the same day as Beethoven's birthday.

**Activities
&
Directions**

1. One easy way to celebrate this day with music is to play any patriotic music, such as *Yankee Doodle* or *Chester*.

2. Another way to celebrate the date is to point out that it is the exact same date as when Beethoven was born. Perhaps you can discuss the interesting phenomenon that Beethoven felt so strongly about freedom and brotherhood. It is interesting to note that his birthday is the anniversary of the day that represented a turning point in the relationship between the colonies and Great Britain.

3. Some of your more dramatic students can dress up like Indians and re-enact the famous scene of swooping down and throwing the tea into the Boston Harbor, with or without Beethoven's *Eroica* Symphony playing in the background.

Winter Winds

Grades: 4-8.

Materials: Recording of "Winter" from *The Four Seasons* by Antonio Vivaldi; picture of a Baroque orchestra (if available).

Concepts:

1. Many composers have written music that is descriptive of seasons of the year.

2. A *tremolo* is produced by rapidly alternating a bow across the string or strings of a stringed instrument.

**Activities
&
Directions**

1. Play part of "Winter" from *The Four Seasons* by Antonio Vivaldi. On the chalkboard, write:

BAROQUE ERA: 1600-1750

Explain that these dates are approximate, but that they are the most widely agreed upon dates. You might then explain that

"Winter" (by Vivaldi) is in the style of composition known as *concerto grosso,* a style which came from the Baroque era. With a receptive class, you can go into more detail, explaining that in this style there are two groups of musicians, one small group and one large, and that for contrast in *dynamics* (the louds and softs of music) these groups are alternated. Music in concerto grosso style usually has a harpsichord giving support to the harmonies.

2. For younger students, many music teachers have found that another approach works well. Have your students imagine a cold winter wind biting through their bodies and ask them what happens. (Do their teeth chatter?) Then listen for the parts of the music that sound like people's teeth chattering, explaining that this is called a *tremolo* and is produced by the string players rapidly alternating their bows across the strings of their instruments. After they are listening attentively, you can have them listen for the two different groups in the concerto grosso and for how some instruments take brief *solos* in which the orchestra gets softer or seems to fade into the background.

Chanukah Celebration

Grades: K-8.

Materials: Recording of the "Chanukah Song" or any other songs available for *Chanukah*; a real *menorah* or pictures of a *menorah*; directions for how to do a *horra* (the dance); the special toy for *Chanukah*, the *dradle*.

Concepts:

1. *Chanukah* is a Hebrew word which means "dedication."
2. *Chanukah* falls at approximately the same time as the Christmas season and is celebrated with gifts, parties, prayer, and the lighting of the *menorah* for eight days.

**Activities
&
Directions**

1. If possible, you might prepare for this lesson by placing a *menorah* in the classroom and lighting a candle for each day of

Chanukah. You can tell the children the story of the miracle in which oil that was supposed to last for only one night lasted for eight nights, which is why candles are lit for eight days. Explain that *Chanukah,* therefore, is known as the feast of lights.

2. Students can have fun in at least two ways: by learning and doing the Jewish dance the *horra* and by playing with the special *Chanukah* toy, the *dradle.* (The *dradle* spins much like a top, and a variety of games can be improvised.) Taste buds can also be brought into the picture if you can obtain the special *Chanukah* pastry known as *levivot.*

3. Many music teachers have found that the "Chanukah song" has great charm and appeal and is learned easily by children. Of course, any song that is appropriate can be used, and many of the traditional songs mention the *menorah* or the *dradle.*

An Opera: Amahl and the Night Visitors

Grades: 3-8.

Materials: Recording of Gian Carlo Menotti's opera *Amahl and the Night Visitors;* a pair of crutches; pictures of the kings who came to see the Christ child (available in many different books); costumes, possibly, so that the kings can be portrayed.

Concept: Although *Amahl and the Night Visitors* has attained great popularity and is shown on television very often, it is an opera in the real sense in that most of the dialogue is sung rather than spoken. (This opera is one of several operas that Gian Carlo Menotti has written.)

Activities & Directions

1. Background for this lesson can be provided by having the students find Bethlehem on the map or by reviewing some of the more important aspects of the story of the birth of the Christ child.

2. An activity approach can involve re-enactment of the story (with the recording), which involves the miracle of a lame boy

being able to walk without his crutches after being hospitable to the kings and wise men who went to see the Christ child.

3. Another approach can be to try to break down the predjudice against opera that music teachers have encountered so frequently. You might do this by asking if the students think of this work as opera. Many might not because it is in English, and there is a common misconception that opera is always in a foreign language because so many are. You can then point out that opera need not be harsh, disagreeable, and hard to understand. The only qualification for opera is that most of the dialogue be sung rather than spoken, and *Amahl and the Night Visitors* qualifies.

An Oratorio: The Messiah

Grades: 3-8.

Materials: Pictures of George Frederick Handel; recording of the entire oratorio the *Messiah* or the famous "Hallelujah Chorus."

Concepts:

1. An oratorio is like an opera, except that there is no staging or costumes. It tells a story, and there are both *arias* (tuneful songs) and sung dialogue called *recitatives*.

2. The *Messiah* was composed by George Frederick Handel, a German Baroque composer (a contemporary of J.S. Bach) who moved to England when he was a young man. Handel started composing oratorios when Italian opera became unfashionable in England.

Activities
&
Directions

1. With younger children, it might be fun not to be too serious and start with the famous "Hallelujah Chorus," doing it the merry old England way, perhaps, and standing when the chorus starts. Background might even be provided by finding Germany on the map and then seeing how one would travel from Germany to England, as Handel did.

2. With older pupils, you can explain that the *Messiah* is a very long work that deals with the prophesy and birth of Jesus, followed by His suffering, His death, and concluding with the resurrection and redemption. Details can be provided such as:

"The *Messiah* is a Christmas oratorio, a work for chorus, orchestra, and soloist."

"The *Messiah* begins with an *overture,* or music heard before the story begins. In this overture there are many *embellishments* (decorative notes added to the music to make it more interesting)."

Pictures of Handel can be shown, showing that his appearance—with powdered wig—was similar to those of some of the founding fathers of the United States.

A Ballet: The Nutcracker

Grades: K-7.

Materials: A tiny Christmas tree or boughs of holly; a recording of *The Nutcracker* (excerpts, the suite, or the full ballet); assorted Christmas toys.

Concepts:

1. Many popular works are more exciting and relevant at certain times of the year (because they were composed specifically to celebrate a holiday).
2. *The Nutcracker* is a ballet performed mainly at Christmas time. A suite was also made using music from the full ballet.

**Activities
&
Directions**

1. *The Nutcracker* is a ballet about a little girl who dreams that her toys come to life and what she will get for Christmas. The story is told through dance, with costumes, to the beautiful music of Tchaikovsky. The specific type of dancing is known as *ballet.* Classical *ballet* uses specific steps or movements, and you might prepare your class by showing pictures of ballerinas or paintings of *ballet* dancers by Degas. Some of your pupils might take

ballet lessons, and you can ask them to demonstrate skills that they have learned in *ballet* class.

2. Another approach is to re-enact a portion of the *ballet* or to extract the essence by setting up the famous scene of a little girl sitting under her Christmas tree. When you read the story to the class, parts can be extracted that your pupils would like to act out, perhaps the "sugarplum fairies" or the "waltz of the flowers." There are filmstrips available that can be shown while the recording is played, and they can help your students decide what other parts of the *ballet* they might like to re-enact.

3. Finally, we hope you will persuade your class to attend a live performance of the ballet or see it on television. Many music teachers look forward to scheduling trips with their classes so that they can see *The Nutcracker* live!

Christmas Carol Songfest

Grades: K-8.

Materials: Recordings of popular Christmas carols, such as "Silent Night," "Deck the Halls," "Jingle Bells," "The Twelve Days of Christmas," and so on.

Concepts:

1. Christmas carols come from many different parts of the world, and most people sing them without being aware of their origin.

2. Caroling is done to bring "glad tidings of cheer" and "good will toward men," thus the moving from house to house (which in a school can be from class to class).

**Activities
&
Directions**

1. As background for this lesson, you might review any of the more famous versions of Christmas. If students are not all from the same ethnic and religious denominations, you might have some of the children compare how they celebrate one of our happiest holidays. Does everyone open gifts on Christmas eve? Are there any unique aspects of how some children's families celebrate Christmas that should be shared?

2. We've had great success not only with singing carols in the classroom, but also with marching around to other classes or through the halls of the school. Of course, you will have to get your principal's approval and the approval of your pupils' parents. But, if you do, the difference will be well worth the effort. Christmas bells to create a more authentic atmosphere can also make a big difference.

3. Another enjoyable activity that many music teachers have found successful is the traditional auditorium "sing." If you can get an entire auditorium singing "Go Tell It on the Mountain" or "We Wish You a Merry Christmas," it will be an exciting morning. Of course, parents can also share the joy if your class can sing at a Parents Association meeting! Then you can set up a small Christmas tree on stage and really have the proper atmosphere.

Sleigh Rides and Snow Maidens

Grades: 2-8.

Materials: Pictures or slides of Eskimos on a dog-drawn sleigh (or sled); sleigh bells; recordings of *Sleigh Ride* by Leroy Anderson and *Snow Maiden* by Rimsky-Korsakov.

Concepts:

1. Both Leroy Anderson and Rimsky-Korsakov were great "orchestrators"—people who have expertise in using instruments effectively.

2. Rimsky-Korsakov was a 19th century composer while Leroy Anderson was a modern, or 20th century, composer. Both used quite large orchestras, especially as compared with the fairly small orchestras of the Baroque era.

**Activities
   &
Directions**

1. Will your students be able to guess that Rimsky-Korsakov was a Russian? They probably will since the name is so Russian sounding. Even children know that much of the U.S.S.R. is Siberia and very cold so Rimsky-Korsakov's *Snow Maiden* will

be quite fitting for the beginning of winter. You might compare it with Leroy Anderson's *Sleigh Ride* and see whether it
also uses sleigh bells. Or you and your class can try to discover
why the composition is called *Snow Maiden*. A related map
activity can be finding Russia on the map of Europe. A multi-
media experience can be provided by showing slides of a sleigh
ride while listening to either composition.

2. Another approach is more historical and analytical. You can
ask your class to compare the size of the orchestra used by
Anderson, or Rimsky-Korsakov, with that used by Vivaldi.
Explain that orchestras grew very much in size during the 19th
century, resulting in late 19th century orchestras that were
very large. Rimsky-Korsakov was such a master at using the
new larger orchestra that he even wrote a famous treatise on
"orchestration."

Sleigh Bells

Grades: K-8.

Materials: Resonator bells; Swiss melode bells; sleigh bells; teacher
desk bell.

Concepts:

1. Some bells are struck with a mallot, others are shook, and still
others are "rung."
2. Almost all "bells" are made of metal.

**Activities
&
Directions**

1. Sleigh bells are employed in many Christmas season musical
compositions, and this might be a good stepping stone to studying bells in general. What is it that they all have in common?
When children draw a bell they usually make the most typcal
bell shape (see Figure 41). But what about door bells or resonator bells? They don't have the typical shape. Swiss melode
bells do have the typical bell shape, and sleigh bells also have
the typical bell shape. We must conclude that there is a bell
family in which some members "look like" bells while others

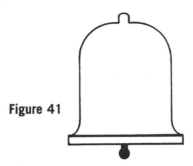

Figure 41

merely "sound like" bells. Why not make these comparisons? Why not have fun comparing the different types of bells.

2. To tie-in with science programs, your students can make a door bell using flashlight batteries. Many books give specific directions. In such a bell, an electric impulse rings the bell. In other types of bells, the ringing is done by hand, either by striking the instrument (resonator bells) or shaking it (sleigh and Swiss melode bells). You might explain that the one thing all bells seem to have in common is that they are all made of metal. But even this is not completely true. Why?

Jingle Bells

Grades: 4-8.

Materials: Piano, miniature organ, or dummy piano keyboard; music for or a recording of "Jingle Bells."

Concepts:

1. The song "Jingle Bells" uses only five different notes: By definition, this is a pentatonic melody.

2. "Jingle Bells" can be played with one hand on the piano, and the five fingers need not be moved out of a basic 1 2 3 4 5 position on the white keys: C, D, E, F, G.

Activities
&
Directions

1. Place Figure 42 on the board. On the piano, place your fingers over the keys as indicated (if the right hand is being used, the

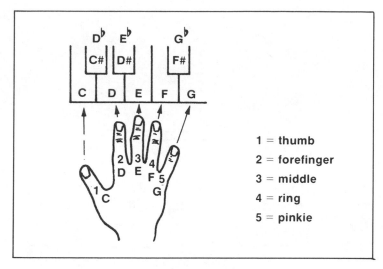

Figure 42

thumb is 1, the pointer is 2, and so on). Then play 3 3 3, 3 3 3, 3 5 1 2 3, 4 4 4 4 4 3 3 3 3 5 5 4 2 1 or E E E, E E E, E G C D E, F F F F F E E E G G F D C. (White keys only are used.)

2. You might also ask the students if they know how many sides a pentagon has. Then relate this to *pentatonic* scales, which have five tones.

3. As many teachers have done in the past, sing this most popular of all the Christmas songs and have lots of fun!

Jolly Old St. Nicholas

Grades: 4-8.

Materials: Piano, miniature organ, or dummy piano keyboard; music for "Jolly Old St. Nicholas" or a recording.

Concepts:

1. The song "Jolly Old St. Nicholas" uses only five different notes. By definition, then, it is a pentatonic melody.

2. "Jolly Old St. Nicholas" can be played with one hand on the piano, and the five fingers need not be moved out of the basic 1 2 3 4 5 position. The five fingers are placed on the black keys of the piano, which are the flats and sharps (C♯ D♯ F♯ G♯ A♯).

**Activities
&
Directions**

1. Place Figure 43 on the board. On the piano, place your fingers on the black keys as indicated (if the right hand is being used, the thumb is 1, the pointer is 2, and so on). Then play:
   5555 444 3333 5   2222 113 43454
   5555 444 3333 5   2222 113 43453

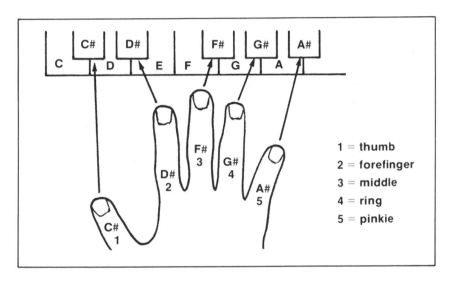

Figure 43

2. Show your students how to do the same thing, and then play and sing the song. Try playing along with a recording. You won't be in the same key, but it will be fun!

Rudolph the Red-Nosed Reindeer

Grades: 2-6.

Materials: Pictures of reindeer; music flashcards; a recording of "Rudolph the Red-Nosed Reindeer."

Concepts:

1. Some Christmas songs are religious in content; others are *secular,* or non-religious.

2. A *syncopation* is like a "musical hiccough." There is a displacement or shifting of the normal accent.

**Activities
&
Directions**

1. Ask your students if they can draw pictures of Santa on his sled and Rudolph with his big red nose. Around Christmas, you can usually find pictures of Rudolph in at least one of the major magazines or comic books. The recording "Rudolph the Red-Nosed Reindeer" can be played in the background and be allowed to "sink in." Some of your students might have children's books that are devoted to "deer" little Rudolph. As the record is played, many of the children will learn the words and start singing along.

2. Some music teachers have found that "Rudolph the Red-Nosed Reindeer" is a good song to introduce the concept of *syncopation* (which means the shifting or displacing of the normal accent). Explain that one sings Ru-DOLF (with the accent on OLF) instead of RU-dolf. Place Figure 44 on the board or music flashcards and point to the accent falling on the second syllable. You can also explain that > is an accent mark. You might also want to try using the first four measures of this song to review eighth, quarter, dotted-half, and whole notes with your class.

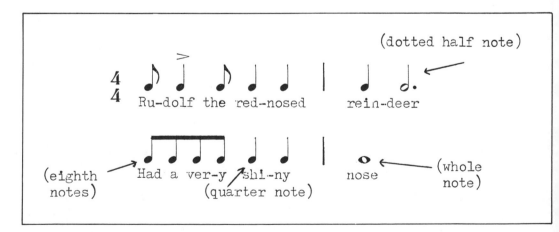

Figure 44

COMPOSERS OF THE MONTH

Happy Birthday Sibelius
(December 8)

Grades: 4-8.

Materials: Recording of *Finlandia* by Jan Sibelius; map of Europe; words and music to "Be Still My Soul," which is based on *Finlandia*.

Concepts:

1. Jan Sibelius was a composer from Finland, a country in the north of Euorpe that is quite cold most of the time.

2. Patriotic songs produce strong feelings.

**Activities
&
Directions**

1. Place on the chalkboard:

    HAPPY BIRTHDAY JAN SIBELIUS
    (December 8, 1865)

    Ask your students what their associations to the date 1865 are. If they don't come up with "the end of the Civil War," you can give them the answer. You might also use a map to locate where Finland is and why it is so cold.

2. To motivate interest in listening to *Finlandia,* many music teachers relate the story of how the tsarist police forbade anyone to listen to it because of the patriotic fervor inspired by the music. Why not listen to the music and see if your class also gets the feeling of nationalism or patriotic pride. Many find the hymn, translated as "Be Still My Soul," one of the most stirring of national anthems. (See Figure 45.)

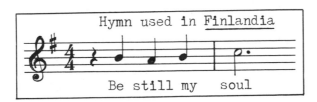

Figure 45

3. When listening to the music, you might also explain that *Finlandia* (using the Finnish national anthem) is a symphonic poem. You might also direct the class's attention to the heavy use of brass instruments at the very beginning of the work. For younger students, you can be much less serious, perhaps, and have fun by letting them listen to the beginning of the composition with their coats on to create the atmosphere of coldness.

Beethoven's Birthday
(December 16)

Grades: 2-8.

Materials: Recordings of Beethoven's Symphony No. 5 in C Minor, the popularized version called "Fifth of Beethoven," and Kodaly's *Hary Janos Suite.*

Concepts:

1. Beethoven is one of the best known of all the classical composers.

2. Beethoven's Fifth Symphony may be the most widely heard of his nine symphonies.

**Activities
&
Directions**

1. On the chalkboard, write:

    HAPPY BIRTHDAY BEETHOVEN
    (December 16, 1770)

    You might give some background to Beethoven's date of birth by pointing out that Beethoven was six years old when the American revolution began and nineteen years old when the French Revolution started. Students can be asked to find Bonn, Germany, on a map of Europe, since Beethoven was born in Bonn. (Capitalize on this alliteration if that sort of thing "gets your students going." Q: "Where was Beethoven born?" A: "Beethoven was born in Bonn.")

2. Clap the rhythmic motive heard at the beginning of the first movement of Beethoven's Symphony No. 5 (three short notes and one long one). You might have the students knock on their

desks in rythmic imitation. Or, perhaps, try to have your pupils guess the opening rhythm by telling them that it is the same as the letter V in Morse code. Tell your students, as many music teachers do, that the opening theme was used as a victory motto during World War II because of *di di di dah* being V in Morse code.

3. You might introduce Beethoven's Symphony No. 5 by first playing "A Fifth of Beethoven," the popularized version of the opening movement of Beethoven's Symphony No. 5. Explain that the opening rhythm is used throughout the movement. Then play the entire first movement of the original Beethoven work. Some music teachers compare repetition in music, art, and fashions in order to develop an understanding of the use of the repetition that occurs in the first movement. For example, the rhythmic motive can be perceived as a pattern that is used over and over for different outfits of clothing. Repetition in painting can be discussed. You might show how the same rhythm is repeated at different levels in the music so that the same rhythm is used but the notes are different.

4. December 16 is also the birthday of Zoltan Kodaly, born 112 years after Beethoven (in 1882). We've had great success with the suite from *Hary Janos*, Kodaly's nationalistic opera. Many children find this Hungarian music quite exciting. Related activities can include finding Hungary on the map and explaining that Kodaly was one of the most important names in music education because he developed a set of hand signals that help teach sight singing.

Puccini's Birthday
Deems Taylor's Birthday
(December 22)

Grades: 2-8.

Materials: *Alice's Adventures in Wonderland* and *Alice Through the Looking Glass*; pictures of Japan or traditional Japanese dress; recordings of Deems Taylor's *Through the Looking Glass* and Giacomo Puccini's *Madame Butterfly*.

Concepts:

1. Both Giacomo Puccini and Deems Taylor were born on December 22 (1858 and 1885).

2. *Madame Butterfly* is an opera and *Through the Looking Glass* is a suite.

**Activities
&
Directions**

1. To create a backdrop for listening to *Madame Butterfly,* your students can locate Japan on a world map or globe, or they can dress up in traditional Japanese clothing. Will your students find it curious that an Italian wrote an opera about Japan? This can lead to a discussion of the opera composer's constant quest for interesting subject matter. When Act One of *Madame Butterfly* is played for your class, will your pupils be able to recognize the "musical quote" from the "Star Spangled Banner"?

2. To create a backdrop for listening to Deems Taylor's *Through the Looking Glass,* the children's books *Alice's Adventures in Wonderland,* and *Alice Through the Looking Glass* can be used. After you explain that the composition is a suite, you and your class can have fun figuring out which of the traditional segments of the well-known story were used in the composition. The record jacket might give you this information.

5

JANUARY

In January children think back on happy thoughts. They return to school refreshed from their Christmas and New Year's vacation. They can remember the joy of Christmas and the presents they received: toys, a sled, a bicycle, new clothing, a game, ice skates. They remember the luxury of getting up late, watching television all day, going to the movies, or just playing with friends. And, of course, the fun of New Year's Eve is still fresh in their minds: making noise, waiting for midnight, and singing "Auld Lang Syne."

January can be a month when you and your class make use of your memories of all this fun! You can recall ice skating with the "Skater's Waltz," the New Year's Day football bowls with music that might have been played at half time, and watching television or movies with continued discussion of television and movie music. You can pay tribute to any days when the children romped in the snow by playing "Musical Snowflakes" or "Singing Snowman."

As in December, there are many musical birthdays from which to choose. We have chosen those of Chabrier, Mozart, Schubert, and Marian Anderson. And there are musical ways of celebrating Carl Sandburg's birthday. So, too, are there many fun-filled ways of commemorating the dates in January on which Georgia, New Mexico, Utah, and Kansas were admitted to the Union as states.

If you don't mind our borrowing a word from December, enjoy a "jolly" January—and don't let the cold get you down!

JANUARY

Figure 46

Grades: 2-7.

Materials: Chalk and chalkboard or music flash cards.

Concepts:

1. Each letter of the alphabet can open up a world of music.
2. The music staff and whole notes as the letter A.

**Activities
&
Directions**

1. Place Figure 46 on the chalkboard or on music flash cards. Ask the children, "What letter does January begin with?" After getting the answer "J," ask the students to name songs, singers, musical instruments, or anything involved with music that begins with J. Add "Jacob's Ladder," the composer Leos Janacek, jazz, the *Jew's Harp* or *jaw harp,* Josquin des Pres (Flemish composer of the 15th century), the Handel oratorio *Judas Maccabeus,* the Juilliard School of Music, Handel's opera *Julius Caesar,* Mozart's *Jupiter* Symphony, Leonard Bernstein's *Jeremiah* Symphony, and the movie music from the film *Jaws* (or any others that you can think of in addition to those elicited from the students).

2. Use Figure 46 to review that the notes have both a rhythmic name ("whole note") and a letter name ("A"). You might review similar lessons for the months of September, October, November, and December. This lesson is much simpler, and it might be a good idea to use it as a point of departure for going back to review these earlier lessons. You can also review the fact that when notes are properly written they look more like footballs than basketballs. Review, also, A through G in music on the five line staff, starting with the A in Figure 46.

Auld Lang Syne

Grades: 2-8.

Materials: Words or music for the song "Auld Lang Syne"; recording of Frank Bridge's composition *Sir Roger de Coverly*, written for Quartet; Scottish kilt or pictures of bagpipe players; piano.

Concepts:

1. The song "Auld Lang Syne" is a Scottish pentatonic melody.

2. "Auld Lang Syne" is associated with the idea that New Year is a time to forget what happened during the past year and start thinking about new things.

**Activities
&
Directions**

1. As background and related activities for this lesson, you can look at pictures of a Scottish bagpipe band, find Scotland on the map, or even look at a real kilt (if one of your students has one). Of course, explain to any child who does not already know it that "Auld Lang Syne" is a song originally from Scotland. To inject some humor, you can write this humorous paraphrase on the chalkboard:

   > "There was a man whose name was Lang
   > And he had a neon sign,
   > And Mr. Lang was very old
   > So they called it old Lang's sign."

2. In the spirit of the new year, you and your class can sing "Auld Lang Syne." You might write the lyrics on the chalkboard or prepare a rexograph sheet. To demonstrate how this song has been used in classical music, play a recording of the composition *Sir Roger de Coverly*, written for Quartet, by Frank Bridge. A discussion can follow about the meaning of "Auld Lang Syne" and why it is sung at midnight on New Year's Eve. You can also explain that many Scottish songs are pentatonic in construction and "Auld Lang Syne" is an example of a pentatonic melody—which leads us to the next part of this lesson.

3. Background for a more complete explanation of the black keys on the piano as a pentatonic scale can be provided by the recording *Blackness* by Rashsaan Roland Kirk (Atlantic

SD1601). This track emphasizes the black keys of the piano. If the recording is not available, show your class that there are only five *different* black keys on the piano, all the rest are duplications at a higher or lower pitch. At this point, you can explain that unlike when you played "Mary Had a Little Lamb" and "Old MacDonald," you might have to use two hands to play "Auld Lang Syne." The reason is that while only five *different* notes are used, we have to use a sixth and seventh pair of notes that are higher versions of the first and second notes (see Figure 47). Thus, the notes for "Auld Lang Syne" can be expressed as:

C♯ F♯ F♯ F♯ A♯ G♯ F♯ G♯ A♯ F♯ F♯ A♯ C♯ D♯ . . . .

D♯ C♯ A♯ A♯ F♯ G♯ F♯ G♯ A♯ G♯ F♯ D♯ D♯ C♯ F♯

Numerically, the song can be expressed as:

1 333 5 434 5 3356 7 . . . .
7 655 3 434 5 3221 3

We suggest that two fingers of the left hand be placed on C♯ and D♯ , preferably the left middle and pointer fingers. Then the right hand can be placed on the remaining five notes, F♯ , G♯ , A♯ , C♯ , D♯ .

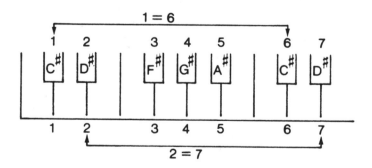

Figure 47

What Did You Do on Your Christmas Vacation?

Grades: 2-8.

Materials: Chalk and chalkboard.

Concepts:

1. Almost everything we do and hear involves music.

2. Music enhances enjoyment of movies and television, in addition to being used for dancing, singing, and listening.

**Activities
&
Directions**

1. List things children did on their Christmas vacation on the chalkboard, checking off those that involved music (such as watching television, going to the movies, hearing radio commercials, dancing, singing in church, and singing around the Christmas tree). Isn't it amazing how much of our lives involves music? You can discuss the role of music as background for movies and television programs and its role in enhancing commercials. In fact, more than 50 percent of all commercials do involve music.

2. Some music teachers can motivate children to make up songs about what they did on their Christmas vacations. The results are fascinating and well worth the effort. It helps, sometimes, to use a music box. If this doesn't work, you might call children up to talk about memorable Christmas experiences that involved singing (such as on Christmas Eve and while gathered around the Christmas tree).

3. Children can also be asked if anyone received a musical toy or musical instrument as a Christmas present: an organ, a guitar, a clarinet, or even a harmonica. Then list them on the board as you did with vacation activities that involved music. List also musical recordings your pupils received as Christmas gifts.

Moods of Movie Music

Grades: 1-8.

Materials: Recordings of movie theme music (preferably current).

Concepts:

1. Music can create feelings of love, sadness, hate, excitement, suspense, and danger.

2. Electronic music often "paints a picture" of outer space or a science fiction plot.

Activities
&
Directions

1. Continue to capitalize on the good feelings your youngsters probably still have about their winter recess for the Christmas and New Year period. Another pleasant memory may be that of going to the movies. You can start a discussion about movies they found particularly exciting. Then ask them how the music contributed to the excitement. You might divide pictures into those about sharks or whales, those about dangerous bears or apes, and those about prehistoric monsters. Many music teachers have good results with love themes from movies; other teachers find that their students talk most readily about movies and movie music involving pets or other domesticated animals. Try to discuss and list as many different moods as you can and play some of the music discussed if available.

2. Electronic music from the movies is a fairly untapped resource that you can put to good use in your classroom. We've had interesting classroom discussions about why electronic music conjures up the vision of outer space and UFO's or an underground, futuristic city. Is it that so many science fiction films have already used electronic music and thus the association is made (just as the Overture to *William Tell* used to stimulate the vision of "The Lone Ranger" or the cavalry charging)? Let's see what conclusions your class comes to.

Skater's Waltz

Grades: 3-8.

Materials: Chalk and chalkboard; record player and recording of the "Skater's Waltz"; tape recorder.

Concepts:

1. "Waltz time" is in 3/4 meter.
2. Ice skating is an enjoyable activity, and it is one that is as closely associated with music as is the *carousel*.

**Activities
&
Directions**

1. To prepare for this lesson, you might discuss ice skating as an activity that some students may have participated in on their Christmas vacation—as part of playing hockey, perhaps, or alone (just for fun). You might take a survey of how many of your pupils ice skate and divide the skaters into those who skate in a rink, those who skate on a lake or pond, and those who skate as part of playing hockey. Some teachers arrange this into a debate as to which is more fun and which is more relaxing. We prefer to emphasize cooperation rather than competition, but competition often produces better results.

2. Another enjoyable activity is to play the "Skater's Waltz" while your pupils close their eyes and think of people ice skating. While the students' eyes are still closed, stop the recording and ask the children to whistle any music they "hear in their heads" as they think of people ice skating. (An optional activity is to tape record this spontaneous whistling, the results of which can be rather "modern" or "contemporary" sounding. Also, while they listen, have students practice the standard conducting pattern for 3/4 meter or waltz time: Down—to the right—up (see Figure 48).

$\frac{3}{4}$ **conducting pattern**

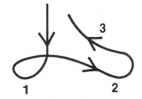

Figure 48

Daytime Television

Grades: 3-8.

Materials: Chalk and chalkboard; a television set (if one is available in the school).

Concepts:

1. Music is a vital part of television program themes and television commercials.

2. Identifying and recognizing musical themes are an important part of musical growth.

**Activities
&
Directions**

1. Ask children questions such as: What programs did you watch on television while you were home in the daytime? Were many of the programs reruns of those you used to watch in the evening? Were some of the musical themes just as exciting as when you first watched the programs? We've found that many students are able to sing, hum, whistle, or clap some of the program themes they heard on programs they watched at home during their vacation. Ask them, and be prepared for a pleasant surprise. While one student sings or whistles a theme, you might have other students try to recognize the music and name the program. As this goes on, you can list some of the programs on the board.

2. Some music teachers have their pupils bring television guides to school and circle the names of programs that have been listed on the board. If a television is available, it would be fun—and nostalgic—to watch some of these programs in class. You can then determine which musical themes are still exciting. Perhaps you can discuss why some program themes are so stirring; what is it about the music—the beat, the rhythm, the scale, the harmonies?

Georgia on My Mind
(January 2)

Grades: 2-8.

Materials: Recordings of "Rainy Night in Georgia" and "Georgia on My Mind"; descriptive literature on Morehouse College and Atlanta University; map of the United States; material on Plains, Georgia.

Concepts:

1. Plains, Georgia, is the home of President Jimmy Carter.
2. There are many songs with names of states in their titles.

**Activities
&
Directions**

1. Place on the chalkboard:
GEORGIA ADMITTED AS A STATE
January 2, 1788

2. A lesson such as this can be started in a variety of ways. One way is to find Georgia on the map and then locate the major cities, such as Atlanta and Savannah. Students in your class can also trace the Savannah River. Another way is to discuss Plains, Georgia, as the home of President Jimmy Carter. You might want to assign some pupils to prepare a report on the American Indian tribes that were indigenous to Georgia, the Creek and Cherokee Indians. It also seems particularly important to mention Morehouse College and Atlanta University, two of the more prestigious institutions of black learning in the United States. Related musical experiences might be playing examples of American Indian music, Negro spirtuals or gospel music, or "Hail to the Chief" and "Ruffles and Flourishes."

3. Among the better known songs that have Georgia in the title are "Rainy Night in Georgia" and "Georgia on My Mind." Explain that "Rainy Night in Georgia" is a "bluesy" song without being in the traditional blues form and play a recording by Al Hibbler or another blues singer who recorded it.

More Cowboy Songs
(January 4)
(January 6)

Grades: K-6.

Materials: Any cowboy songs available (on recordings or in song books); cowboy outfits; Chinese temple blocks or pictures of Chinese temple blocks.

Concepts:

1. New Mexico and Utah were part of the Wild West that we often read about or see in the movies.
2. Many so-called cowboy songs have a Mexican influence.
3. Oddly enough, the instrument that often gives the characteristic "horse hoof" sound is called the *Chinese temple block*.

**Activities
&
Directions**

1. Place on the chalkboard:

   UTAH ADMITTED AS A STATE
   January 4, 1899
   and
   NEW MEXICO ADMITTED AS A STATE
   January 6, 1912

2. Ask your students if they know what musical instrument makes the sound of horse hoofs. It is probably a rhetorical question, because it is rare that students (or even teachers) know the answer. It should probably be called the cowboy something-or-other, but it isn't. Oddly enough it is the *Chinese temple block*. This sound may be illustrated best in "On the Trail" from the *Grand Canyon Suite* by Ferde Grofe. Although it is not listed in "Materials," many music teachers use this selection to illustrate the sound of the temple blocks, and you might want to use it also. If you can obtain a real set of temple blocks, you'll find that they are most fun to play. Your class will love them.

3. You can play cowboy songs in the background ("Cool Water," "Don't Fence Me In," "Tumblin' Tumbleweed," and so on) while a variety of activities take place. Younger children can dress up as cowboys and cowgirls and play with toy horses, covered wagons, and so on. Older students might find Utah and New Mexico on the map, contrast their locations with that of "the Grand Canyon State," Colorado, and discuss the climate and deserts of these states. With intellectually gifted students you might even discuss the problem of indigenous Americans and how they were treated in the history of our nation. What, for example, are current conditions on Indian reservations? Also, discuss the Mormon settlement of Utah.

Marian Anderson's Birthday
(January 5)

Grades: 2-8.

Materials: Recordings of art songs and spirituals, sung by Marian Anderson.

Concepts:

1. Marian Anderson is a world-renowned black, female contralto born in Philadelphia, Pennsylvania, in 1902.
2. A contralto voice is deeper than a soprano voice.

**Activities
&
Directions**

1. Marian Anderson was the first black American to sing in an opera at the Metropolitan Opera House in New York City in 1955. With older students you might discuss the question of why it took so long after the Civil War and the Emancipation Proclamation for such an event to take place. On the chalkboard, write:

   HAPPY BIRTHDAY MARIAN ANDERSON
   (January 5, 1902)

   Some teachers even relate her being born in the "city of brotherly love" and the home of the Liberty Bell to her role as a champion of freedom in the arts.

2. Additional details about Marian Anderson can be provided. You might tell your students that she made her debut in Berlin, Germany, in 1933. Older students might appreciate this phenomenon, since Hitler was rising to power at the time. You might play one or two examples of her singing German art songs by Franz Schubert. A particular favorite of ours is her rendition of Schubert's *Erlkonig* (The Erl King). This lesson can even be related to Schubert's birthday, which occurs on the 31st of this month.

3. A recording of Marian Anderson singing spirituals would be very enjoyable for this date. It is marvelous to hear spirituals being sung by such a well-trained voice! Many music teachers find that in recent years what used to be well-known spirituals are no longer familiar to children.

Happy Birthday Carl Sandburg
(January 6)

Grades: 3-8.

Materials: Pictures of Carl Sandburg and Abraham Lincoln; copies of any of the volumes of Sandburg's biography of Abraham Lincoln; recording of the *Lincoln Portrait* by Aaron Copland.

Concepts:

1. Carl Sandburg is probably best known for his biography of Abraham Lincoln.
2. A musical "miniature biography" of Abraham Lincoln is the *Lincoln Portrait* by Aaron Copland.

Activities & Directions

1. Older children can be provided with details about Carl Sandburg's biography, such as the titles of specific parts of the biography: *The Prairie Years, The War Years,* and so on. They might also be interested in the famous Lincoln-Douglas debates. (Some teachers are particularly successful at structuring debates. You might want to try assigning research projects regarding the Lincoln-Douglas debates so that debate topics are accurate.) Younger children might be interested in some of Abe Lincoln's humor, such as his answer to the question "How long should a man's legs be?" (His answer was, "Long enough to reach the ground.")

2. Another enjoyable activity is to listen to Aaron Copland's *Lincoln Portrait* with an eye toward learning about Lincoln's life. How much can children learn from this musical composition? You might point out how the music at the very beginning of the work seems to be calling: A-bra-ham. Oh, A-bra-ham. At any rate, comparisons can be made as to how both literature and a descriptive musical work can depict aspects of a great man's life.

Football Frolic
(Throwing in Rhythm)

Grades: 3-8.

Materials: Footballs; replica of a football field, with goal posts.

Concepts:

1. 2/4, 3/4, and 4/4 meters.
2. Musical notes look more like footballs than like basketballs.

Activities
&
Directions

1. The idea of beats being *grouped* in "twos," "threes," or "fours" is one that has led music-theory teachers to use terms such as *duple* and *triple* meter. An activity that can be fun and help develop the concept of beats being "grouped" is as follows. Group students into "twos," "threes," and "fours"; i.e., two students together in a group, three students together in a group, and four students together in a group. Have them toss a football and count out loud, so that you hear, ONE two, ONE two three, or ONE two three four. We've had success using this approach because it's fun for the children. It's not a chore, but there is an important musical concept involved. Another enjoyable way of thinking in terms of "twos," "threes," and "fours" is to take two, three, or four throws to make a goal. You might play this game by placing three children between "the 50 yard line" and a "touchdown," for example, with three throws being allowed to score.

2. Another football frolic activity can be to use seven different footballs, naming them A, B, C, D, E, F, and G for the musical alphabet. You can then either make up words (BAD, CAB, and so on), as is often done with the musical alphabet, or make up two teams of "line notes" versus "space notes" (F A C E versus E G B D F). You and your students will probably think of many variations of such games.

Football Half Times

Grades: 2-7.

Materials: Recordings of college songs often associated with football bowls (Rose Bowl, Cotton Bowl, and so on, such as the Navy or Notre Dame fight songs; recordings of famous marches such as those by John Philip Sousa; football uniforms and pictures of pro football teams (or outstanding college teams).

Concepts:

1. Most college bowls and super bowls have exciting half-time shows that feature very fine marching bands.
2. Marching bands require members who can both march well in formation and read music with great ease.
3. In marches *beats* are grouped by twos or fours, such as ONE two, ONE two or ONE two three four, ONE two three four.
4. On New Year's Day there are many football games and many marching bands in parades.

Activities
&
Directions

1. One way to start this lesson is by asking your students how many of them watched football half times, especially on New Year's Day and Superbowl Sunday. Then you can tell them to prepare for their own marching-band half time. Either they or you can try planning some basic formations or simple marching steps. Draw from your own experiences, perhaps, for simple drills such as "at ease," "ten-hut," "bout face," "to the rear," or "column right." With whatever patterns you have designed, play a recording of college songs or John Philip Sousa marches and practice your own marching band formations. Older students can use real instruments, and younger students (second and third grade) can use toy instruments. After some practice, you might discuss the importance of facility in both playing and marching, especially when difficult formations are being performed or executed.
2. Another important aspect of this lesson is learning about 2/4

and 4/4 meters, or "march time." You can explain that the *meter* of marches is two or four beats grouped together. A number of activities can provide the experiential background, or "Education as Experience." Students can clap loudly on the accented beats and lightly on the unaccented beats, trying to determine whether the particular march played is in 2/4 or 4/4. Help students determine how many weak beats were heard before the strong beat was clapped for the second time and tell your students that strong and weak accents help us determine the meter of a composition. You might have the students march while saying ONE two three four, ONE two three four or ONE two, ONE two. You can try practicing an about-face on the fourth beat of 4/4 (for example, LEFT right left TURN, LEFT right left TURN). It might be interesting to divide the class into those who say ONE two three four and those who say LEFT right left TURN, so that they are going on simultaneously: ONE/LEFT two/right three/left four/TURN. It might also help to write 4/4 on the board and explain that the top four means that there are four beats in every measure and the bottom four means that each quarter note gets one beat.

Stephen Foster Memorial Day
(January 13)

Grades: K-8.

Materials: Any of the many Stephen Foster songs, such as "Old Folks at Home," "Camptown Races," "My Old Kentucky Home," "I Dream of Jeanie With the Light Brown Hair," and "Oh! Susannah."

Concepts:

1. Stephen Foster had almost no formal musical training.

2. Most Foster songs are in the major mode (which can be described to beginners as the C major scale without any sharps or flats).

3. Although he was "born on the fourth of July" in the best American tradition, Stephen Foster died in relative poverty on January 13, 1864. January 13 was later declared "Stephen Foster Memorial Day."

**Activities
&
Directions**

1. It is always interesting when a great American is born on July 4, the day of American Independence. One wonders how, if at all, this affected his career of writing songs that more than anyone else's embody the "typical" American-sounding melody. It is also interesting to note that he wrote most of his famous so-called minstrel or "Ethiopian" songs long before he ever journeyed South, although it is said that he heard "the singing of Negroes on the wharves of the Ohio River." You might start this lesson by writing on the chalkboard,

   STEPHEN FOSTER MEMORIAL DAY
   January 13

   Then you can mention that he was born in Pittsburg, Pennsylvania, find Pittsburg on the map, and trace the Ohio River.

2. Play several Stephen Foster songs and ask your students if there seems to be any commonality. If anyone says "they all seem to sound the same," you might mention that they are all in a *major key.* The sound of a major key can be demonstrated by playing C D E F G A B C on the piano or on easy-to-play instruments such as the resonator bells.

3. It might be fun to try to figure out some of the songs below. We'll give you the beginning notes, and you can try to figure out the rhythms and titles. Don't look at the answers until you've tried *very hard!* Then try them out on your students and see if they know the songs (*cover the answers with a blank page*).

#1

C B C G   E

(Answer: BEAUTIFUL DREAMER)

#2

C E F G   GG A C B A G

(Answer: OLD FOLKS AT HOME)

#3

C D E E C DE FEFA G

(Answer: MY OLD KENTUCKY HOME)

#4

G A G E D C C A

(Answer: MASSA'S IN THE COLD, COLD GROUND)

#5

GG EG AG E

(Answer: CAMPTOWN RACES)

#6

```
                      A
            G   G         G
        E                     E            EE
     D                            D      D        D
  C                            C              C
```

(Answer: OH! SUSANNAH)

Musical Snowflakes

Grades: 1-4.

Materials: Paper cutouts of snowflakes; chalkboard; music flash cards.

Concepts:

1. Games can help children learn to identify lines and spaces of the trebel staff.
2. We can spell words with the musical alphabet on the staff.

Activities
&
Directions

1. Make paper cutouts of snowflakes. Place them on the five lines and four spaces of the treble staff so that they spell words such as "bee" and "cabbage." (See Figure 49.) You can also spell the basic spaces and lines of the staff, as in Figure 50.

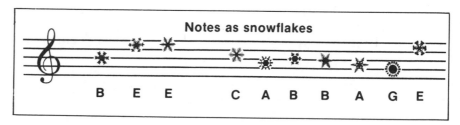

Figure 49

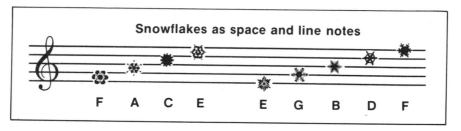

Figure 50

2. Distribute music flash cards and paper snowflakes. Show children what fun it is to try to spell words such as "ace" or "bed." Then give small prizes to the students who spell the most words or choose up teams that compete against each other. ADDITIONAL WORDS: egg, be, deed, dead, ad, add, fee, feed, fed, gage, babe.

Going to Kansas City
(January 29)

Grades: 3-8.

Materials: Recording of "Everything's Up to Date in Kansas City" from *Oklahoma* or the continually popular "shuffle blues" song known as "Going to Kansas City."

Concept: Prior to the Civil War, the state of Kansas was known as "Bleeding Kansas."

**Activities
&
Directions**

1. You might take a discovery approach as to whether the song from the broadway musical *Oklahoma* refers to Kansas City, Kansas, or Kansas City, Missouri. The same applies to the fairly familiar blues, "shuffle rhythm" song "Going to Kansas City." With older students you can discuss the political situation in "Bleeding Kansas" prior to the Civil War. Why was Kansas admitted as a state right before the Civil War—or had the Civil War already started?

2. The song from *Oklahoma* "Everything's Up to Date in Kansas City" was considered riské in its time. Why? Listen and find out.

3. The song "Going to Kansas City" also seems to suggest the idea of Kansas City being a really *swinging* place! By all means, don't get carried away in school, but you might allude to minstrel shows or French cancan dancing such as one often sees in the movies.

4. You might point out that the composer Delius was born on the same date as when Kansas became a state. Then place on the board:

KANSAS ADMITTED AS A STATE
January 29, 1861

Singing Snowman

Grades: 3-6.

Materials: Snowman costume.

Concepts:

1. Many songs have been written about winter, snow, and snowmen.

2. Making up songs is enjoyable as well as creative.

**Activities
&
Directions**

1. Prior to this lesson, you might announce that you will be having a singing snowman contest. At home, or both at home and in school, the children will make snowman costumes. Small awards can be given to the best outfit, in anticipation of the grand prize for the best singing snowman. We've found it necessary to prepare for this exercise in creativity. You might discuss the process of creativity as sometimes being no more difficult than putting new words to a familiar tune or a new tune to familiar words. Many children (and, indeed, many adults) believe that creativity cannot be taught (nor bought, but *can* be caught, and should be sought!). You need not teach falsely that creativity is *very* easy. But you can help change the notion that only few people can be creative in music.

2. In the actual "singing snowman" contest, first ask for volunteers to start off the game. If children don't volunteer readily, play familiar songs in the background, such as "Frosty the Snowman." If it turns out that your students are more bashful than you thought, you may have to guide combining bits and fragments of familiar songs so that the end result is a different song. One silly combination is "I'm dreaming of Frosty the Snowman with a very shining nose, and you'd better not pout when he comes our way with his sleigh." Think up an interesting prize for the winner of this contest—and a good booby prize also.

COMPOSERS OF THE MONTH

Happy Birthday Chabrier
(January 18)

Grades: 2-8.

Materials: Pictures of flamenco dancers; castenets; recording of *España*, a rhapsody for orchestra by Emanuel Chabrier.

Concepts:

1. Many non-Spanish composers have been fascinated with Spanish music.

2. A *rhapsody* is a free form composition that is loosely constructed.

Activities
&
Directions

1. Preparatory activities for listening to *Espana* can be locating Spain on the map, trying to use the castenets, and looking at pictures of flamenco dancers. Some student or students in your class might even be able to do flamenco dancing, or at least try.

2. Tell students that since Chabrier is pronounced Cha-bree-ay, it rhymes with birthday! Students who are amused by rhyme will be delighted with,

HAPPY BIRTHDAY, CHABRIER
(January 18, 1841)

It might be fun to sing "Happy Birth-day Cha-brier" with castenents.

3. Many music teachers have found that *Espana* can be used with great success. The music has a very exciting flavor, and it is great fun to try to count all seven melodies in the work. Students can also make believe they are visiting Spain from France, jotting down Spanish melodies in a notebook, and then later working the melodies into a loosely connected work called a *rhapsody.* (Do you know any other composers who wrote music inspired by Spain? Answer: Rimsky-Korsakov and Debussy.)

Mozart's Birthday
(January 27)

Grades: K-8.

Materials: Recording of "Twinkle, Twinkle Little Star" or the music; recording of Mozart's Twelve Variations in C Major on the French folk tune "Ah vous dirai-je, Maman" K. 265.

Concepts:

1. Many songs we know are quite old. "Twinkle Twinkle Little Star" was originally a French folksong called "Ah, vous dirai-je, Maman."

2. Mozart, the great Austrian composer, used many different forms in music. One of them is called theme and variations.

**Activities
&
Directions**

1. Most young children can sing "Twinkle, Twinkle Little Star." It is the type of song that is learned on one's mother's knee. After singing this familiar song in class, play Mozart's set of 12 variations. You might not want to tell your students what it is at first. Let them be surprised that it is a song they know. Ask them if they knew that it was originally a French folk tune. Let them listen to the entire recording and ask them to describe the music. You may be able to elicit a good definition of the variation form instead of giving them a ready-made definition.

2. Another approach is to play the Mozart variations without first singing the song. Ask your pupils to raise their hands when they hear a familiar melody. Then have them raise their hands each time the melody is changed. Then you can tell them that this changing of the melody is called a variation. Afterwards, try singing "Twinkle, Twinkle Little Star" with some variation. Are any students able to do this well? Will any be able to sing "Happy Birthday" to Mozart with some variation of the melody? Write on the chalkboard:

HAPPY BIRTHDAY WOLFGANG AMADEUS MOZART
(January 27, 1756)

Note: Mozart died in 1791 at the very young age of 35.

Schubert's Birthday
(January 31)

Grades: 3-8.

Materials: Chalk and chalkboard; recordings of Schubert's *Winterreise* (Winter's Journey) and *Erlkonig* (The Erl King).

Concepts:

1. Any day can be the birthday of a famous composer.

2. Many famous composers wrote "cycles" of songs about a central theme. One of Schubert's cycles is a "Winter's Journey."

3. During the winter months, people must move quickly to stay

warm. In "The Erl King," Schubert depicted moving quickly in music.

**Activities
&
Directions**

1. Place on the chalkboard:

   HAPPY BIRTHDAY FRANZ SCHUBERT
   (January 31, 1797)

   As background for listening to the art songs, you can ask your students how many years ago Franz Schubert was born (a mathematical activity). Or ask students if they can guess where Schubert was born. (Answer: Vienna, Austria.) Then use a map to find the location. Students might also be interested in the very sad fact that just as he was born on the 31st of the month. Schubert died at the age of 31! Yet he wrote over 1,000 compositions! Many music teachers also point out that although Beethoven and Schubert never met, Schubert died a year after Beethoven died (1827 and 1828), and today their graves exist side by side.

2. We've found that children are enthralled with *Erlkonig*. In the first place, it is very relevant for winter listening. The story is about the Erl King riding on a horse, in winter, with his dying child. Moreover, the singer has to portray not one, but three characters. You might have your students raise their hands when the singer's voice changes to portray a different character. We recommend the Marian Anderson recording. Can your students write their own poems with three or more characters? When you're listening to this famous art song, don't forget to direct pupils' attention to how the music depicts the horse moving quickly through the snow.

3. *Winterreise,* or "Winter's Journey," is another Schubert composition particularly relevant for a January listening activity. You can point out that art songs are musical settings of poems by poets who are considered great (as opposed to rhymes written by songwriters.) A song "cycle" is a series of songs with a central theme. Some teachers try to get their classes to write several poems about the winter and how they feel about the winter. Then you can play one or several of the songs from the cycle known as "Winter's Journey" (such as "Numbness," "The Linden Tree," and "Good Night").

6

FEBRUARY

What a diverse month February is! It is filled with love (Valentine's Day and Brotherhood Week), revelry and religiousness *(Mardi Gras and Dia de la Candelaria)*, ethnic celebration (Chinese New Year), birthdays of important composers, and birthdays of two of our greatest presidents (George Washington and Abraham Lincoln). All of these events can be celebrated musically, which shows that music is everywhere and in everything!

If you like alliteration, you could nickname February "Mardi Gras Month" or even "Marmot Month" since February 2 is Ground Hog Day or Woodchuck Day (and ground hogs are sometimes called marmots). If you want to get rid of the winter doldrums, "Marmot Month" may be right up your alley; after all, the marmot may *not* see his shadow, which would mean that you *would not* have to wait six weeks for spring.

February is also Afro-American History month, which contains Black History Week—both of which can be tied-in musically and historically to Lincoln's Birthday and the Emancipation Proclamation. Even Washington's Birthday can be tied-in since he willed his slaves to be free at his wife's death. Oddly enough, one of the greats of gospel singing, Mahalia Jackson, died two days before the month of February, on January 27, in 1972.

Great composers abound in February: Victor Herbert, Mendelssohn, Alban Berg, Chopin, Handel, Carpenter, and Rossini. We have chosen to include birthdays of Victor Herbert, Chopin, Rossini, and Mendelssohn. How can you help but enjoy February musically? We will do everything to make sure you will.

139

February

Figure 51

Grades: 1-8.

Materials: Chalk and chalkboard; music flash cards; music or recordings that begin with F; actual instruments whose names begin with F, such as the flute or flutophone.

Concepts:

1. Words can be spelled on a staff by substituting musical notes for the actual letters.

2. The middle line of the treble staff is B, and the note right below it in the second space is A. The top line is F, and the note right below it in the fourth space is E.

Activities
&
Directions

1. Place Figure 51 on the chalkboard or music flashcards. You might point out that the very first note is F whole note, the next is E half note, and the next is B quarter note. Your students should already know whole, half, and quarter notes. If not, we suggest explaining that in 4/4, or common time, a whole note gets four beats, a half note gets two beats, and a quarter note gets one beat. Note also that between U and R we placed a single eighth note, which is an A (in the second space). This eighth note in 4/4 time would receive a half of a beat. With younger children in particular review the fact that the note is filled in, has a stem or line, and has a flag.

2. We've had great success asking students to use the beginning letter of the month to name singers, songs, or instruments. In addition to those elicited from the students, such as flute or flutophone, add and write on the board: Falla (the composer), falsetto (a way of singing), *Falstaff* (the opera by Verdi), *Fantas-*

tic Symphony (by Berlioz), Fanfare (usually played by trumpets), Faure (the composer), *Fidelio* (the opera by Beethoven), the fife (small flute), and *Fingal's Cave* (an overture by Mendelssohn).

National Freedom Day
(February 1)

Grades: 3-8.

Materials: Songs using the theme of freedom or the quest for liberty such as "We Shall Overcome," "Lift Every Voice and Sing," and "Oh Freedom"; patriotic songs such as our national anthem, "God Bless America," and "America the Beautiful."

Concept: The United States of America stands for freedom, although there are still minorities that do not have financial freedom in the fullest sense.

**Activities
&
Directions**

1. Ever since Patrick Henry said, "Give me liberty or give me death," America has stood for freedom. It is the land of the free, the land that welcomed the hungry masses yearning to be free. You might even mention the prerevolutionary era of William Penn and his quest for religious freedom. Songs such as "We Shall Overcome" or "Lift Every Voice and Sing" can be sung today, in addition to standard patriotic songs such as our national anthem, the first verse of which ends with "o'er the land of the free...."

2. Many music teachers have found that the song "This Land Is Your Land" by Woody Guthrie is particularly meaningful and symbolic of freedom for all races, religions, and creeds. You can sing it (it is very easy) or listen to one of the many recordings of the song.

Ground Hog Day
(February 2)

Grades: K-8.

Materials: Recordings of, or words and music to, songs about spring such as "Spring Is Here" or "It Might as Well Be Spring."

Concepts:

1. If the ground hog sees his shadow on Ground Hog Day, there is another six weeks of winter—or another six weeks before spring.

2. A pleasant *Candlemas* means a cold spring.

**Activities
&
Directions**

1. Ground Hog Day falls on *Candlemas.* An old church tradition maintains that a pleasant Candlemas means a cold spring, and this belief probably gave rise to the ground hog legend. You might assign older students to investigate this topic. They could bring in reports on *Candlemas,* exploring exactly what it is and whether it is one of the holidays borrowed from pagan rituals. Younger students might obtain some of the many cute pictures of ground hogs that proliferate around this date.

2. Maybe the ground hog won't see his shadow and warm weather will come soon to take you out of the winter blahs. To reinforce this "positive thinking," we've played songs such as "Spring Is Here" or "It Might as Well Be Spring." Children are often optimists; you can be, too!

Dia de la Candelaria
(February 2)

Grades: K-8.

Materials: Pictures of bulls and bullfights; recording of Aaron Copland's *El Salon Mexico;* recording of the Mexican Hat Dance ("La Raspa"); recordings of the Tijuana Brass; pictures of Mexico City.

Concepts:

1. All of Mexico celebrates *Dia de la Candelaria* with dances, processions, and bullfights.

2. Much of Mexican traditional music is in 6/8 time.

Activities & Directions

1. Background and correlation with social studies can be provided by the following information about "Our Southern Neighbor." Many children know about the conquest of the Aztecs by the Spanish conquistadors, headed by Cortez. You might add the legend of how Mexico City was founded when an Aztec tribe saw an eagle perched on a cactus protruding from a stone while devouring a snake. Later, the original name of *Tenochtitlan* ("cactus on a stone") was changed to Mexico in honor of the Aztec war god Mexitli. This explanation can be followed by pictures of Mexico City. With older students you might be able to discuss the terms *mestizo* and "wetback" (which might provoke controversy) and the liberation of Mexico by Benito Juarez after the French forcibly seized Mexico and placed Maximillian (of the House of Hapsburg) on the throne.

2. Younger children will love to do the Mexican Hat Dance to celebrate this event. We've successfully used recordings of the Tijuana Brass and various recordings of bullfight music (including the "Toreador Song" from *Carmen*, although it represents the Spanish rather than Mexican bullfight). You can also play Aaron Copland's *El Salon Mexico* and point out that much of Mexican traditional music is in 6/8 meter. When playing the "Toreador Song" or authentic Mexican bullfight music you can show bullfight pictures from a book or from posters, which are often available from travel agencies.

February Fingers

Grades: 2-6.

Materials: Piano; chalk and chalkboard.

Concepts:

1. *Staccato* is an Italian word used in music. Literally it means a knife, but in music it means sharp and short.
2. *Presto* is a "tempo" indication meaning quickly.

3. The most common tempo and dynamic signs in music are in Italian.

Activities
&
Directions

1. Here's an activity that is as much a game as a keyboard experience. Tell the children that *presto* means quickly in Italian and then ask your students to line up at a piano *presto!* Then explain that you want them to imagine that the piano keys are so icey cold or hot that when they touch them they no sooner press them down than they are forced to pull their fingers away quickly or *presto*. One at a time, students will press down one or two keys and pull their fingers away, saying "ouch!" as if they were icey cold or burning hot.

2. You can deal with the concept of *staccato* in the same way. Explaining that *staccato* is short and sharp, demonstrate a short and sharp attack on one of the piano notes. Then ask the children in line to do it. You might have fun by having them say "February Fingers" as they try a *staccato* attack.

3. Another approach is to make two lines. One line will be the "presto players" and the other the "staccato stingers." Starting with an equal number of students in each line, which line will play a note and get back to their seats the fastest? You might even tape record the entire thing! You might get some very interesting atonal effects, plus the shuffling of feet and giggling.

Brotherhood Week

Grades: K-8.

Materials: Words and music or recordings of songs such as "There Is a Brotherhood of Man," "It's a Small World," I'd Like to Teach the World to Sing," "Let There Be Peace on Earth," "United We Stand," and *Donna Nobis Pacem* (Grant Us Peace).

Concepts:

1. During Brotherhood Week, many extra attempts, from interfaith services to ecumenical councils, are made to bring people together.

2. Syncopation in music is a shifting or displacement of the normal accent.

Activities
&
Directions

1. The United States became a great nation because of contributions made by people who have different cultural backgrounds. Although the "melting pot" concept has in recent years been replaced by an "ethnic diversity" concept, you might sing or listen to the song "United We Stand" to symbolize this great idea.

2. For Brotherhood Week you can't beat a song that contains the word "brotherhood" in its title—and the song from the Broadway show *How to Succeed in Business Without Trying* "There Is a Brotherhood of Man" does just that. Many music teachers use this song as an example of *syncopation*. Note that there's an *eighth rest* at the beginning of many lines creating a syncopated accent on the first word (see Figure 52).

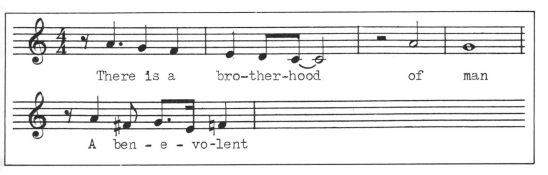

Figure 52

3. Other songs have been found to be particularly enjoyable by young people. Among them are: "It's a Small World After All" (used as the theme for the 1964 World's Fair in New York City) and "I'd like to Teach the World to Sing" (which originally was a Coca Cola commercial). One line in "I'd Like to Teach the World to Sing" is "I'd like to see the world for once, all holding hand in hand. . . ." Both songs are particularly meaningful and relevant for Brotherhood Week. Since brotherhood also implies peace, there are two other songs that we and other music teachers have been successful with—"Let There be Peace on Earth" and *Donna Nobis Pacem*. *Donna Nobis Pacem* is a traditional round that some children know. "Let There Be Peace On

Earth" is a fairly recent song that really caught on in school situations. We recommend both highly.

Afro-American History Month

Grades: K-8.

Materials: Ragtime music of Scott Joplin or Eubie Blake; Harry Belafonte calypso records; ballads by Nat "King" Cole; big band music of Duke Ellington or Count Basie; recordings of all black Broadway musicals such as *The Wiz* and *Bubbling Brown Sugar;* recordings of 1950's rock 'n' roll music by Chubby Checker and Fats Domino.

Concepts:

1. Black Americans have made extraordinary contributions in the field of music.
2. In this country, people of African descent have variously been called colored, Negro, Afro-American, and, most recently, black.

Activities
&
Directions

1. The movie *The Sting* helped popularize ragtime music, although the ragtime revival had already started. We find that students of all ages love ragtime. You might want to use video tapes of Eubie Blake playing and explaining ragtime. Also available are video tapes of Gunther Schuller and the New England Conservatory playing ragtime music.
2. The number of black contributions to music in this country is just incredible. In almost every field of music (most recently in classical music with Leontyne Price, Martina Arroyo, and others), the famous black performers are too numerous to mention. Just take your pick, from Eubie Blake and Scott Joplin at the turn of the century, to Aretha Franklin, James Brown, Charley Pride, and Michael Jackson in more recent years. Play whatever you want—your choice here.
3. Many calendars and almanacs list Afro-American History Month; others list Black History Week. We included Afro-American History Month because the emphasis is on American as much as on Afro. Many of the analogies between African

music and what happened to it in this country defy musical analysis. The music is new and unusual, being a unique blend of African and American vitality.

Black History Week
(Lesson #1)

Grades: K-8.

Materials: Words and music to, or recordings of, "Lift Ev'ry Voice and Sing" and "We Shall Overcome." Recording of the famous Martin Luther King speech "I Have a Dream"; pictures of the civil rights marches of the 1960's.

Concepts:

1. Black History Week is usually observed in February (and ties in nicely with Brotherhood Week, National Freedom Day, and Washington's and Lincoln's Birthdays).

2. Sometimes Black History Week is expanded into Afro-American History Month (see the previous lesson), giving more time to study contributions that black Americans have made in all fields.

Activities & Directions

1. One of the great speeches of all time, "I Have a Dream," was given in Washington, D.C. by Dr. Martin Luther King, Jr. It provides wonderful motivation for an exciting kick-off lesson. You might follow this up with bulletin board displays or films and filmstrips. Many of the films of the protest marches that resulted in great gains for blacks in this country contain the powerful and moving song "We Shall Overcome." Please teach it to any student who is not yet familiar with the song. It is quite short and easy to learn:

> We shall overcome,
> We shall overcome,
> We shall overcome someday
> And deep in my heart,
> I do believe,
> That we shall overcome someday.

2. The official song of the NAACP (National Association for the

Advancement of Colored People), "Lift Ev'ry Voice and Sing,"
is harder to learn but worth every minute of effort. It is sometimes called on written music the Negro National Hymn. It
ends with the words, "Let us march on 'til victory is won." This,
of course, can be related to the marches of the 1960's. The
song is very beautiful, and we recommend it highly.

Black History Week
(Lesson #2)

Grades: 2-8.

Materials: Recordings of spirituals sung by Martina Arroyo, Paul
Robeson, Leontyne Price, and others; recording of *Spirituals
for Orchestra* by Morton Gould.

Concepts:

1. Many spirituals were created by slaves to be sung at their religious services.
2. Spirituals were originally sung *a cappella*. *A cappella* means unaccompanied singing (without any instruments).

**Activities
&
Directions**

1. In preparation for this lesson, you might listen to any recordings you obtain to be sure you find ones that are *a cappella*.
Many spirituals were originally sung unaccompanied but in
recent years have been arranged with piano or orchestral ac-
companiment. This fact can be illustrated with Morton Gould's
Spirituals for Orchestra. Listen to this work to see how many
spirituals you can identify. Then play it for your class and see
how many of the spirituals your students recognize. With older
students, you might go on to a general discussion of slavery or
discuss the fact that most spirituals deal with biblical passages
or the desire to find peace in the afterlife. Flying up to heaven,
getting on the train, crossing the river Jordan, climbing up the
ladder—all figure prominently in spirituals. What other details
can your students add?
2. If you are using recordings by Martina Arroyo or Leontyne
Price, you might want to mention their roles as stars of the
Metropolitan Opera in New York. If you are using a recording

by Paul Robeson, you may or may not want to relate the tragedy of his being blacklisted in the 1930's because he was a communist and that he eventually went to Russia to live.

3. Many teachers differentiate between spirituals that are for solo voice and those that are for soloist and choir. If any of the spirituals you use are for soloist and choir, comment on the "leader and response" form.

Black History Week
(Lesson #3)

Grades: 2-8.

Materials: Recordings by Mahalia Jackson, including such songs as "He's Got the Whole World in His Hands," "Just a Closer Walk with Thee," "Nearer My God to Thee," and "Move on Up a Little Higher"; pictures of Mahalia Jackson.

Concepts:

1. Gospel music is another important aspect of the black experience.
2. Born in New Orleans (like Louis Armstrong) in 1911, Mahalia Jackson was a black vocalist who was well known for singing gospel music.

Activities
&
Directions

1. "Mahalia was *melismatic*" is a catchy little phrase that students like to repeat with a variety of inflections, sometimes emphasizing the "m" sound, sometimes holding the "is" part of the word. We've found that it works quite well in leading to a fuller explanation of the word *melismatic* and how it applies to Mahalia Jackson's singing. In Mahalia Jackson's singing, she often sang not only the melody note, but also the notes above and below. This is what *melismatic* means, turns and flourishes on a sustained syllable, and this is one aspect of gospel music. Listen for this aspect of her singing as you play a Mahalia Jackson recording and point it out to your students whenever it occurs. The use of handclapping to emphasize the "after-beats" of 2 and 4 and the use of tambourines are other aspects of gospel you can listen for.

2. Like Louis Armstrong, Mahalia Jackson was born in New Orleans. Students can locate New Orleans, Louisiana, on the map,
and you can discuss the influences New Orleans had on jazz,
blues, gospel, ragtime, minstrel, and gospel. Discuss the Creole
culture, perhaps assigning older students to write reports on
the topic. Has anyone ever heard the *patois* of the Creole
French spoken or been to the Bayou country?

Lincoln's Birthday
(February 12)

Grades: 1-8.

Materials: Pictures of Abraham Lincoln; recording of Aaron Copland's
Lincoln Portrait; books about Lincoln or copies of the Gettysburg Address; pictures of the Lincoln Memorial.

Concepts:

1. Abraham Lincoln was the 16th President of the United States
and was in office during the Civil War.
2. Aaron Copland's *Lincoln Portrait* is for orchestra and narrator.

**Activities
&
Directions**

1. Background and preparation for this lesson can involve looking at pictures of Lincoln, the Lincoln Memorial, or even the
Battle of Gettysburg (Lincoln made his famous Gettysburg
Address in Gettysburg). Older students can read some of his
famous speeches, such as the Gettysburg Address; then they
can listen for excerpts from these speeches when they hear
Copland's *Lincoln Portrait.* You might also have the students
find Springfield, Illinois, where Lincoln was born, on a map of
the United States. Making a list of cities, counties, buildings,
music centers (e.g. Lincoln Center in New York), colleges, and
so on that bear Lincoln's name is also fun. The list is almost
endless!
2. When playing the *Lincoln Portrait,* you can tell your students
that many famous people have been the narrator for this piece.
This being Afro-American History Month, you might inform
your students that Marian Anderson (who once proclaimed

that if she couldn't sing at the Metropolitan Opera she would sing on the steps of the Lincoln Memorial) has served as narrator for this famous work.

Born on the Fourth of July!

Grades: K-8.

Materials: Pictures of Louis ("Satchmo") Armstrong; recordings by Louis Armstrong (preferably one that includes "Dixie," "When the Saints Go Marching In," "Just a Closer Walk with Thee," or "Hello Dolly").

Concepts:

1. Louis Armstrong was among the black musicians who were not only nationally prominent but also internationally known.
2. Louis Armstrong's style of trumpet playing was known as "swing" or Dixieland.

**Activities
&
Directions**

1. It is interesting to note when a very great American is born on the 4th of July. Does the person work harder to live up to the birthdate? Why not discuss this with your class. If the children are too young to discuss this interesting phenomenon, you might want to teach them the George M. Cohan song "I'm a Yankee Doodle Dandy," in which he mentions ". . . a real live nephew of My Uncle Sam, born on the fourth of July." Or sing a well-known song by Stephen Foster, also born on July 4th, followed by "When the Saints Go Marching In," a song often sung by Louis Armstrong.

2. Many music teachers emphasize that Louis Armstrong (July 4, 1900-July 7, 1971) was born in New Orleans, Louisiana, a city that some consider the birthplace of jazz. They describe and show pictures of the funeral marching bands. You can play "When the Saints Go Marching In" or "Just a Closer Walk with Thee" to illustrate this. They show pictures of "Satchmo" and include recordings such as "Hello Dolly," in which he both sings and plays. They discuss his many trips around the world as a goodwill ambassador. Young children will love to imitate

his famous broad smile and the handkerchief that he always carried in his hand to wipe either his trumpet or the perspiration from his brow.

Valentine's Day
(February 14)

Grades: 3-8.

Materials: Love songs such as "Love Is a Many Splendored Thing," "More," "We've Only Just Begun," "Close To You," "The Look of Love," "Til There Was You," "When I Fall in Love," "I Love You," and, of course, "My Funny Valentine"; red construction paper and scissors; chalk and chalkboard or music flash cards.

Concepts:
1. The symbol for Valentine's Day is a red heart.(See Figure 53.)
2. The idea of love has inspired thousands of songs and musical compositions.

Figure 53

Activities
&
Directions

With any of the beautiful songs listed in "Materials" in the background, here's an activity that is fun for Valentine's Day and helps teach music reading. Get red construction paper and have students cut out red hearts. You can place the hearts on music flash cards to spell simple words (see Figure 54) or outline a song such as "My Funny Valentine" with hearts (see Figure 55).

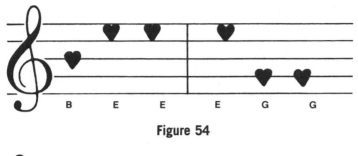

Figure 54

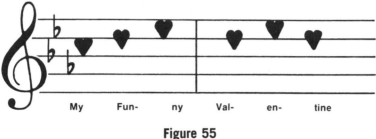

Figure 55

Liszt's Love and A Lonely Heart

Grades: 3-8.

Materials: Construction paper and other materials needed to make Valentine's Day cards; recordings of Tchaikovsky's "None But the Lonely Heart" and Liszt's *Liebestraum* ("A Dream of Love"); books of love poems.

Concepts:

1. On Valentine's Day, it is traditional to give Valentine's Day cards, which often read, "Be My Valentine."

2. *Liebestraum* (a nocturne for piano) and "None But the Lonely Heart" are classical compositions dealing with love.

**Activities
   &
Directions**

1. On Valentine's Day, a tour of elementary school classrooms around the country would find many students busily making Valentine's Day cards for their mothers or girl friends. Why not use some of the beautiful poems that one finds in books of love poetry? Older students might write their own poems. In

addition to containing the words "Be My Valentine," each Valentine's Day card would contain a beautiful poem.

2. As the students work, Liszt's beautiful *Liebestraum* or Tchaikovsky's "None But the Lonely Heart" can be played in the background. You might want to point out that both seem to be sad songs of love rather than songs rejoicing in a shared love. You might even inspire some of your students to set their poems to music, making an art song instead of a popular song. Of course, you and your students may not be able to write the song down, but it is a creative act nevertheless. You can even use the melodies from *Liebestraum* and "None But the Lonely Heart" for your original poems.

Let's Harp on Love!

Grades: K-8.

Materials: Pictures of the harp; pictures of Cupid with his arrows and lyre; recordings mentioning heartstrings, such as "Zing Went the Strings of my Heart."

Concepts:

1. The harp is a stringed instrument that is a "visitor" rather than a regular member of the orchestra.

2. The harp has often been symbolic of love, and it is probably the sound of the harp that is envisioned when the term "heartstrings" is used.

Activities
&
Directions

1. Show pictures of the harp or of the harp being played and play recordings that mention the harp or use terms such as "strings of my heart" and "heartstrings." You might ask your students to think of movies and television programs in which a man sees a pretty girl and one immediately hears the sound of a harp!

2. Often, pictures of Cupid are also shown at these times, and we sometimes hear the "plunk" of Cupid's arrow. We've found, also, that children love to draw the heart with the arrow through it or to try to draw Cupid himself.

The Grand Canyon
(February 14)

Grades: K-8.

Materials: Pictures of the Grand Canyon; recording of Ferde Grofe's *Grand Canyon Suite*.

Concepts:

1. "On the Trail" was once used for a Phillip Morris cigarette commercial.
2. The Grand Canyon is in Arizona.
3. The *Grand Canyon Suite* was written by Ferde Grofe.

**Activities
&
Directions**

1. If you have not yet used the *Grand Canyon Suite* as a listening activity, you can use this composition to commemorate the day on which Arizona was admitted as a state. Of course, this is also Valentine's Day, and you may want to use the *Grand Canyon Suite* for this day's listening activity only if you cannot locate love music. Or you can do both, dividing your listening lesson in half—half love music and half music to commemorate Arizona's becoming a state. Pictures of the Grand Canyon would be welcome, of course, and your students could also locate it on a map. For fun, before writing *suite* on the board, you might ask your students if they want to hear some *suite* (sweet) music!

2. Place on the chalkboard:

ARIZONA ADMITTED AS A STATE
February 14, 1912

Fat Tuesday

Grades: K-8.

Materials: Festive dress; recordings of *Creole Dance Suite* by Alberto Ginestera, *Brazilian Impressions* by Ottorino Respighi, the movie score from *Black Orpheus, Carnival* by Dvorak, *Carnival Jest* by Schumann, the fourth movement of Ravel's *Rap-*

sodie Espagnole, Dixieland music from New Orleans; slides or pictures of places that have *Mardi Gras* or *Carnival,* such as New Orleans, Mobile (Alabama), Trinidad, Rio de Janeiro (Brazil), Quebec City (Canada), Rome, Venice, Milan, Naples (Italy), Paris (France); words and music for "Alouette" or "Frere Jacques."

Concepts:

1. In French, *Mardi Gras* means "fat Tuesday." Places following the French tradition use the term *Mardi Gras.*

2. *Carnival* comes from Latin (*caro,* "flesh," and *vale,* "farewell"). Places following the Latin or Roman tradition use the term *Carnival.*

3. In some places the terms *Mardi Gras* and *Carnival* are synonymous and interchangeable.

Activities
&
Directions

1. In Roman Catholic communities, the period of revelry immediately preceding Lent is called *Mardi Gras* or *Carnival.* The custom is believed to be a survival of *Saturnalia,* an ancient Roman celebration. The Roman Catholic festival originally extended from January 6, the feast of the Epiphany, through Shrove Tuesday. This period was eventually restricted to a week or so by the Popes, who disapproved of the riotous festivities. In France, carnival was further confined to Shrove Tuesday (part of *Shrovetide*), hence the term "fat Tuesday." On the other days of *Shrovetide* (days immediately preceding Ash Wednesday) the chief activities were being "shriven" or confessing. After people were "shriven," a period of amusement followed which lasted until Ash Wednesday or the beginning of Lent. Some of your students may know some of this information. Older students can be assigned this topic for individual or group reports.

2. As one activity, you can show slides or pictures of places that have *Mardi Gras* or *Carnival*, and then students can try to locate these cities. Because of the differences in climate, you might discuss how temperature can affect the ways in which *Mardi Gras* can be celebrated in New Orleans or Trinidad as opposed to Paris or Quebec City. Slides or pictures can show, for example, the day and night revelry that takes place in the streets of

Rio de Janeiro and Trinidad (because of the warmth). You can show pictures of dancing in the streets and parades, or even re-enact the tradition of crowning a King and Queen of the *Carnival.*

3. As a tribute to the *Mardi Gras* in Quebec City, you might sing "Alouette." For the *Mardi Gras* in Paris, you can sing "Frere Jacques." Children particulary love touching their noses, and their chins while they sing "Alouette." For *Carnival* in Italian cities, you might do the dance the *tarantella.* Have any of your students been to festivals—particularly in Mobile, New Orleans, or Quebec City? What a thrill it will be if one of your students saw a festival in Europe or South America!

4. We've listed enough compositions (see "Materials") for you to play one every day of the festival period. All of them are exciting, jubilant music because they reflect the revelry of celebration prior to the sober Lent period, during which Catholics are supposed to deprive themselves of something they enjoy.

Chinese New Year

Grades: K-8.

Materials: Pictures of the festivities that go on during the Chinese New Year, such as the dragon both worn and carried by several people; resonator bells or piano.

Concepts:

1. Chinese New Year usually falls in February.
2. Most old Chinese melodies are pentatonic; i.e., they use only five different notes.

Activities & Directions

1. If you've ever seen filmed segments of the festivities that go on during the Chinese New Year (especially in New York and San Francisco), you know that children would love to re-enact some of them. In fact, the fireworks and firecrackers that we use for the Fourth of July are inspired by the Chinese celebration. You might consider using sparklers, since they are the least dangerous of all fireworks and are usually legal. But the activ-

ity that your students might enjoy most is one in which a dragon head with a hollow body is carried around, several children having the hollow body over their heads. If you can obtain one or make one, you will insure a fun day!

2. Figure 56 is part of a Chinese lullaby ("The Purple Bamboo")
that is an old folksong using only five different notes (pentatonic). We've changed it to "no sharps or flats" to make it
even easier to play on the piano or resonator bells. We hope
you can play this lovely little tune (it uses only half, quarter,
and eighth notes). Your students can whistle it, perhaps while
they carry around the dragon you've made (if you've been able
to make one).

Figure 56

Washington's Birthday
(February 22)

Grades: 1-8.

Materials: Slides and pictures of places that have the name
Washington; recordings of Charles Ives's "Washington's
Birthday" from his *Holidays Symphony* and excerpts from
the musical *1776.*

Concepts:

1. George Washington was the first President of the United States
and is called the Father of our country.

2. Washington D.C. is named in memory of George Washington.

3. Both *Holidays Symphony* and *1776* are examples of 20th Century music.

**Activities
&
Directions**

1. Have students find Washington D.C. on the map and tell them that this city was named in memory of George Washington. You could also show slides and pictures of the Washington Monument and other places that have the name Washington. Students could list places, institutions, buildings, centers, bridges, and so on that have the name Washington. You might even sing "Happy Birthday" to Washington—especially if you forgot to do it for Lincoln on his birthday.

2. Listening to excerpts from the broadway musical *1776* or Ives's *Holidays Symphony* (the "Washington's Birthday" section) should be fun. Both are exciting, lively pieces of 20th Century music—neither one will put your students to sleep.

COMPOSERS OF THE MONTH

Victor Herbert's Birthday
(February 1)

Grades: K-8.

Materials: Assorted toys, especially toy soldiers or any toys that can be "marched"; recordings of Victor Herbert's "March of the Toy Soldiers" from *Babes in Toyland,* his Suite for Cello and Orchestra, and his Concerto for Cello and Orchestra; pictures of the cello; map of Ireland or the British Isles.

Concepts:

1. Victor Herbert was a famous cellist as well as a composer of many operettas, such as *Babes in Toyland.*
2. The cello is a member of the string family of the orchestra.

**Activities
&
Directions**

1. As we've often suggested, you can start by placing on the chalkboard,

HAPPY BIRTHDAY VICTOR HERBERT
(February 1, 1859)

singing happy birthday, discussing his date of birth in relationship to when the Civil War started, and finding his birthplace (Dublin, Ireland) on the map.

2. Victor Herbert was a cellist, and his Suite for Cello and Orchestra and his Concerto for Cello and Orchestra highlight the cello as a virtuoso instrument. Pictures of the cello can be shown while you listen to either of these works. A live demonstration of the cello would be preferable. If neither of these recordings is available, you might use his most famous piece, the "March of the Toy Soldiers" from his operetta *Babes in Toyland.* Young children always love this work, and, of course, they can have fun by sitting on the floor "marching" their toys around as you play the music.

Mendelssohn's Birthday
(February 3)

Grades: 3-8.

Materials: Someone's wedding album (your own or one of your student's parents'); recordings of Mendelssohn's incidental music from *A Midsummer Night's Dream* and "War March of the Priests" from *Athalia* (or *Athalie*); copy of Shakespeare's *A Midsummer Night's Dream.*

Concepts:

1. Felix Mendelssohn wrote many compositions that are well known by most people, and equally important, he was responsible for rediscovering the music of Johann Sebastian Bach (which was neglected after Bach's death).

2. Many great composers wrote "incidental" music for famous plays, which was played at various times during the play or between acts.

Activities
&
Directions

1. Write on the board:

HAPPY BIRTHDAY FELIX MENDELSSOHN
(February 3, 1809)

Point out that Mendelssohn was only four years old when he
started piano lessons in 1813 (the same year that both Verdi
and Wagner were born). On the map, students may locate
Hamburg, Germany, where he was born. Don't forget to laugh
about the fact that the hamburger was conceived of in, and
named after, Hamburg, Germany. (Can you give out tiny
hamburgers to your class?)

2. Older students might read Shakespeare's play before you play
Mendelssohn's incidental music. Tell your class that they wll
hear several melodies in this work, but one tune will be particularly well known. Students can raise their hands when they
hear it (the "Wedding March"), and you might discuss later
whether they can recall hearing it at a wedding they've attended. They might enjoy looking at a wedding album, especially if it's yours!

3. The "War March of the Priests" is another composition that
many music teachers use, and it is often used as a graduation
march. Has it ever been used at your school?

Chopin's Birthday
(February 22)

Grades: 1-8.

Materials: Stop watch; recordings of Chopin's "Minute" Waltz in D Flat
(Opus 64, No. 1), if possible both as a piano solo and as a
vocal solo by Barbra Streisand; recording of Chopin's
Polonaise ("Military") in A (Op. 40, No. 1); Chopin's Nocturne in E Flat Major (Op. 9, No. 2).

Concepts:

1. Chopin died young at 39 (although not quite so young as
Schubert, who was 31, or Mozart, who was 35).

2. A *polonaise* is a Polish dance in 3/4 meter.

3. *Nocturne* means "night music."

Activities
&
Directions

1. Place on the chalkboard,

HAPPY BIRTHDAY FREDERICK CHOPIN
(February 22, 1810)

Students can locate his birthplace (Poland) on the map. If you play the "Military" Polonaise and begin to hear the strong ONE two three, ONE two three of the polonaise, you might want to try singing "Happy Birthday" in that manner. Another enjoyable activity is to dance the polonaise. All that is necessary is that the boys and girls line up in separate lines and then hold hands and lift them over their heads their hands still held together. With their hands held high, they begin to march ONE two three, ONE two three, which normally doesn't seem like a march. But as they "march" around the room, the feet are alternated as follows: LEFT right left, RIGHT left right. When you hear the music you will know what we mean.

2. The *nocturne* (night music) is soft and soothing. Children love to put their heads down on their desks when they are quite young and to write poems inspired by the music when they are older. On the other hand, an exciting and amusing activity is to use a stop watch to "time" the "Minute" Waltz—either a piano version or the vocal solo sung by Barbra Streisand.

Born on Leap Year: Rossini's Birthday
(February 29)

Grades: 1-5.

Materials: Toy bows and arrows; recording of the overture to *William Tell* by Rossini.

Concepts:

1. Born on February 29, 1792, Gioacchino Rossini was born on a leap year.

2. The overture to *William Tell* was used for *The Lone Ranger* radio series and is usually recognized as such by children.

**Activities
&
Directions**

1. Place on the board:

HAPPY BIRTHDAY GIOACCHINO ROSSINI
(February 29, 1792)

On a map, children can either locate Italy, where Rossini was born, or Switzerland, where the William Tell story takes place. This is a good background activity. Even more fun is to ask the children what is wrong with the information on the board. See how long it takes before someone discovers that usually there is no February 29! Of course, first and second graders may have to do it orally if they cannot read well. You might go over the saying, "Thirty days has September. . . ."

2. We've had great success with re-enacting the portion of *William Tell* in which the father must shoot an apple off his son's head in order to save his life. (Use rubber-tipped "suction" arrows.)

3. When you play the overture to *William Tell*, see if any of your pupils recognize the portion that was used for the radio series *The Lone Ranger*. Because of the recent interest in nostalgia, at least one student will probably exclaim: "That's *The Lone Ranger* music!

7

MARCH

Spring will soon be here! And what fringe benefits we get in March: St. Patrick's Day, Japanese American Week, the day New York City saw the first bicycle being used. (And it's the Persian and Roman New Year!) A wonderful assortment of colors and flavors can be in store for those who make use of all the possibilities—from green cookies and clothing to exotic Japanese and Persian culinary delights.

There certainly is no shortage of "composers of the month": Debussy, Ravel, Hovhaness, Barber, Rimsky-Korsakov, Honegger, Mussorgsky, Bartok, Villa-Lobos, Quincy Jones, Jr., and none other than the great Johann Sebastian Bach himself! We have included lessons on Villa-Lobos, Ravel, Rimsky-Korsakov, Bach, Mussorgsky, and Haydn.

States admitted to the Union during March were Ohio, Nebraska, Vermont, and Florida. During the spring the *moonlight in Vermont* that inspired the song of the same name must be even more beautiful than ever; the same for the moon over the Ohio River.

Swing into spring and really enjoy it. We do!

March

Figure 57

Grades: 2-8.

Materials: Chalk and chalkboard or music flashcards.

Concepts:

1. Each letter of the alphabet can open up a world of music.
2. The musical staff and eighth notes.
3. Music notes can have lines, or stems, that go down on the left side or up on the right side.

Activities
&
Directions

1. Place Figure 57 on the board or on music flash cards. Say to the children, "What letter does March begin with?" After getting the answer "M," ask the children to name songs, singers, musical instruments, or anything involved with music that begins with M. To those answers elicited from the students, you might add MacDowell (19th century American composer who wrote *Indian Suite*), the opera *Madama Butterfly*, madrigal (the 14th and 15th century nonreligious song form), Mahler, Mendelssohn, Manhattan School of Music, Mason (Lowell Mason, one of the earliest American composers, born in 1792), Massenet, Metropolitan Opera, Meyerbeer, Milhaud (20th century French composer), *Military Symphony* (by Haydn), Monteverdi, *Moonlight Sonata,* Mozart, musicology, and Mussorgsky.

2. Have you taught your students eighth notes yet? If not, point out that Figure 58 contains two eighth notes—one with the stem going up on the right side and the other with the stem going down on the left side. We have found that students never forget the "A" and "C" in M A R C H, perhaps because it

Figure 58

is a five letter word. Since E I G H T H has only six letters, maybe they will also "always remember" what single eighth notes on the musical staff look like.

Trains and Steamboats
(March 1)

Grades: K-5.

Materials: Map of the United States; pictures of corn fields, steamboats, railroad trains or toy steamboats, and model trains; recording of "Rock Island Line" and "Oh What a Beautiful Morning."

Concepts:

1. Songs, such as "Rock Island Line," have been written about trains and railroad systems.

2. Many songs allude to corn fields.

**Activities
&
Directions**

1. To commemorate Nebraska's entry as a state in 1876, you might play the well-known folk song "Rock Island Line." The Rock Island Line is one of the five great railroad systems in the large state of Nebraska. A related map activity can be tracing the Nebraska River or the Missouri River and their many tributaries. Younger children can use toy trains as you play a recording of "Rock Island Line." We have also found students to be fascinated by the Pony Express that traveled through Nebraska on route from Missouri to California.

2. To commemorate Ohio's entry as a state in 1803, you might try to get a recording of "Beautiful Blue Ohio" or the Ohio State

University song. More readily available, however, is the song "Oh What a Beautiful Morning" from the Broadway show *Oklahoma*. This song would be relevant because Ohio is one of the corn states, and one of the lines in the song is "... the corn is as high as an elephant's eye." This line usually makes younger children giggle, which is a wonderful sound in this sometimes all too serious world. Older students can also trace the Ohio River, which after the Mississippi and Missouri Rivers is probably the largest in the country. Note also that the steamboat made Cincinnati a great river port, and younger students can look at pictures of steamboats or play with toy ones.

Bicycle Built for Two
(March 1819)

Grades: K-5.

Materials: Recording of "Bicycle Built for Two"; pictures of bicycles, tricycles, and the "gay nineties" bicycles built for two.

Concepts:

1. Along with songs such as "Daisy, Daisy," "Take Me Out to the Ballgame," "And the Band Played On," the famous "Bicycle Built for Two" is the type of song known as a *sing-along*.
2. "Bicycle Built for Two" is a waltz in 3/4 meter.

**Activities
&
Directions**

1. Why not have a *sing-along*? There are many slides and filmstrips available of songs usually associated with sing-alongs. One of these songs is "Bicycle Built for Two." Of course, if your principal gives you permission, you can spice it up by having pupils bring their bicycles (or tricycles in the younger grades) to school.
2. Related discussion can center around March 1819 being the time New York City saw its first bicycle, and you can show pictures of the two seater bicycles used that inspired the song.
3. Younger students will have to be taught the words by rote, of course, or the slide or filmstrip can be used as material

for teaching reading. Older students can have their attentions called to the fact that this is still another waltz (which is in 3/4 meter), although it is more commonly used as a sing-along than a dance number.

4. Additional discussion might center around the fact that while some people use their bicycles during winter, ice often prevents frequent use and it is spring which finds more frequent use of bicycles.

March in Miami
(March 3)

Grades: 2-8.

Materials: Recording of *Florida Suite* by Frederick Delius; pictures of Disneyworld, the Everglades, alligators, crocodiles, pelicans, beaches in Miami, Seminole Indians; materials on Ponce de Leon and his quest for the fountain of youth.

Concepts:

1. In March 1513, Ponce de Leon led a search for the fountain of youth.
2. The English impressionist Frederick Delius wrote *Florida Suite.*

Activities
&
Directions

1. Since March is said to "come in like a lion" and "go out like a lamb," you might think about the weather at this time in Miami Beach—especially if you are still experiencing chilly March winds. You might show pictures of Disneyworld and alligators, crocodiles, and pelicans in the Everglades. Have any of your children been to these places? Has anyone seen Seminole Indians wrestling with alligators?

2. The *Florida Suite,* by Frederick Delius, is an impressionist composition that can quite easily make your students think of lying on the beach (a welcome thought if you are tired of cold weather) or travelling through marshes and swamps. This can easily lead to a discussion of how the Spanish navigator Ponce de Leon, then Governor of Puerto Rico, led an expedition in

March 1513 in search of the fountain of youth. Oddly enough, he landed on March 27, on Easter Sunday. We have often discussed this coincidence and the fact that his expedition was in March, the same month of Florida's entry as a state. Ask your students if they think Florida was purposely admitted as a state in March (March 3, 1845) because of it being the month of Ponce de Leon's expedition. After some lively discussion, return to the *Florida Suite* and listen more carefully to the way that the music presents impressions of a warm climate and a sometimes tropical atmosphere.

Moonlight for March
(March 4)

Grades: 3-8.

Materials: Recording of "Moonlight in Vermont"; pictures of the Green Mountains of Vermont or Vermont marble.

Concepts:

1. Vermont means green mountains in French.

2. Vermont is famous for winter sports and as a year-round resort state.

3. The great beauty of Vermont obviously inspired the well-known song "Moonlight in Vermont."

Activities
&
Directions

1. The following information can provide a background for listening to "Moonlight in Vermont." Vermont seems to have been first explored by Samuel de Champlain, who, in 1609, journeyed to the lake that bears his name. (Your students might trace this route.) The beauty of the Green Mountains, which some compare in beauty to the Swiss Alps, led to the area being called Vermont (French for green mountains). Have your pupils locate them.

2. We've had great success in motivating interest with the story of Ethan Allen and the Green Mountain Boys. They captured

Fort Ticonderoga on May 10, 1775. This was the first aggressive act of the War of American Colonists, after Vermont proclaimed itself independent of New York. Later, Vermont became the 14th state, soon after the original 13, in 1791. Many music teachers have found that patriotic music is appropriate here. Pupils can re-enact the capture.

3. Pictures of the Green Mountains or Vermont's famous marble works create great interest. A piece of real marble can be used. You might even teach the class to chip marble while listening to "Moonlight in Vermont."

Happy Persian and Roman New Year

Grades: 3-8.

Materials: Pictures of the guitar, sitar, and (if possible) the Persian *tar*; map that includes the ancient Roman and Persian empires; guitar.

Concepts:

1. The tar, which is still played by Iranian musicians, might be the forerunner of the guitar and the sitar.
2. Present day Iran was ancient Persia.

**Activities
&
Directions**

1. Exoticism is fascinating to many children. How interesting that March, the month of the Vernal Equinox or the first day of spring, was for both the ancient Persians and Romans the beginning of the new year. The exact name of the Persian (now Iranian) new year's day holiday is *NoRuz*. It is a national holiday that is very colorful, reaching back into the shadows of time (possibly as early as 4500 B.C.) and featuring seven foods, all starting with the Persian letter S (sepand, or wild rice; seeb, or apples; serkeh, or vinegar; seer, or garlic; samanu, or malt paste; sabzeh, or green vegetables; and sumac, or herbs). You can also tell the students that March is named after the Roman war god Mars, who was also in charge of vegetation. Since March is the start of the growing season, it seems to make sense

that this would be the first month or new year. The Romans, too, had big festivals at this time, so if you want to have a party in class, go to it!

2. At your Roman and Persian new year's party you can play guitar or sitar music in the background—being sure, of course, to point out that the Persian *tar* came before both of these instruments. It is difficult to find recorded *tar* music, but perhaps if you look real hard. . . . For your students who like rhyme, call it a "Persian party."

Winter Wind

Grades: 4-8.

Materials: Chopin's Etude in A Minor, Op. 25 ("Winter Wind").

Concepts:

1. Op. is an abbrevation for *opus* (meaning work or composition in Latin, but usually applied to the order of publication of a composer's compositions).
2. *Etude* is a French word for a study or practice lesson to increase a performer's technical ability.
3. Chopin's Etude in A Minor, from his Opus 25 (twelve studies), has been called the "Winter Wind" *etude*.

Activities
&
Directions

1. It has been said that March "really lets you have it" before it's over—another way of saying that it comes in like a lion and goes out like a lamb. Of course, the lion part is the March winds, and the lamb part is the coming of spring. For the lion part, we have used a recording of one of Chopin's *etudes,* or studies. It has been called his "Winter Wind" *etude,* and if you play it you will probably understand why. Many of the notes move quickly and *chromatically* (by half steps), sounding like the March winds. Why not place the title on the board without its nickname and ask your students for their impressions.

2. You might also refer to all those pictures of the wind that are so familiar to children; for example, the ones of clouds with

cheeks puffed (Is that Mr. North Wind?). Talented artists in your class might be able to draw an impression of a combination lion-and-wind.

St. Patrick's Day
(March 17)

Grades: K-8.

Materials: Drum; words and music or recordings of the songs "My Wild Irish Rose" and "When Irish Eyes Are Smiling"; green construction paper or cookies.

Concepts:

1. St. Patrick's Day is observed on March 17. On this day people of Irish descent in America parade and celebrate.
2. The *upbeat* or *pickup* gets its name from the upward motion of the orchestra conductor.

Activities & Directions

1. As background for St. Patrick's Day activities, your students might be interested in the story of St. Patrick (who was probably born in Scotland!) being sent by the Pope to the Emerald Isle, where he drove the snakes away by beating on a drum. Younger students might particularly enjoy re-enacting this story. On this day, also, students can wear green and bring a shamrock if a parent has one. Or, you can cut out shamrocks from construction paper and serve green cookies or cookies with green frosting on them. Additional background activities can include finding Ireland on the map, talking about contributions to literature by Irish Americans (you might want to use F. Scott Fitzgerald because of the popularity of *The Great Gatsby),* and having your own St. Patrick's Day parade.
2. Older students can learn that some of the best-known Irish waltzes, such as "When Irish Eyes Are Smiling" and "My Wild Irish Rose," begin on an upbeat (see Figure 59). You might place a diagram for a 3/4 or waltz pattern on the board and explain that the term upbeat takes its name from the fact that

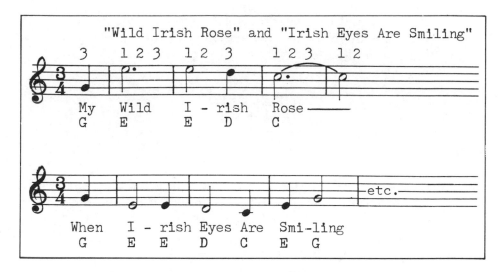

Figure 59

the third motion of the 3/4 pattern is UP (down, right, up), and thus the third beat is the *upbeat.* The same is true, of course, of the fourth beat in the 4/4 pattern.

Building a Bagpipe

Grades: 3-7.

Materials: Knapsacks or duffle bags; pipes and reeds.

Concepts:

1. Bagpipes use reeds that vibrate.
2. The shorter the length of tubing the higher the pitch; the longer the length of tubing the lower or deeper the pitch.

**Activities
&
Directions**

1. Ask students to bring old knapsacks or duffle bags to class. Explain that the object of this activity is to place tubes of different lengths in holes that are made in the bags. The places where the tubes are inserted must not leak. Have students experiment with the apparatus in several ways:

a. Use instrument mouthpieces (clarinet, trumpet, saxaphone, and so on) at the point of blowing, or

b. Build the bagpipe so that a reed is forced to vibrate at the end of the inserted tubes as the air tries to escape when the "player" blows into one of the pipes, or

c. Build the bagpipe so that there is some combination of vibrating reeds either at the point of blowing or at the ends of the inserted tubes.

2. You might also plan some reward for the student or students who succeed in building a bagpipe that works. Reward students who systematically investigate the science of how to build a working bagpipe.

SALUTE TO SPRING
OR
SWING INTO SPRING

Mussorgsky and Bach were both born on March 21, and March 21 is Earth Day, which usually falls on the first day of spring. But sometimes spring begins on March 20—when the Vernal Equinox occurs on that date. What a great topic for a science lesson! What follows is but a small portion of what can be done on and around the beginning of spring. If it was a particularly bad winter, we bet you're quite glad spring has begun—even if your students had lots of fun with their snowballs and winter sports.

Appalachian Spring

Grades: 4-8.

Materials: Recording of *Appalachian Spring* by Aaron Copland; pictures of Appalachia.

Concept: Many well-known composers use folk tunes in their major works.

Activities
&
Directions

1. The song "Simple Gift" was sung by the Shakers. The song starts out " 'Tis a gift to be simple. . . ." and is a well-known

Shaker hymn. Do any of your children know it? It was used by Aaron Copland in *Appalachian Spring,* a ballet about 19th century pioneers who had a spring celebration around their new farmhouse in the hills of Pennsylvania.

2. A background or related activity can be to look at pictures of Appalachia in Pennsylvania and find it on the map.

Spring by Different Composers

Grades: K-8.

Materials: Recordings of Rubinstein's *Melody in F,* Respighi's "Spring" from his *Trittico Botticelliano* or Botticelli Tryptich, *To Spring* by Edvard Grieg, *Spring Song* by Mendelssohn, the "White Peacock" from *Roman Sketches* by Charles Tomlinson Griffes, "Spring" from the *The Four Seasons* by Vivaldi; pictures of birds—including the peacock; baseball caps and bats.

Concepts:

1. Trills and tremolos are often used in music to imitate birds.
2. Spring is the season when grass, trees, and flowers begin to grow.
3. Many people like to greet spring because the cold weather is over.
4. Many different kinds of birds can be seen during the spring.

**Activities
&
Directions**

1. Listen to Respighi's "Spring" and notice how the colors of the orchestra seem to "break out" or "burst forth" like fireworks! One of the ways that this great orchestrator has achieved these effects is by using trills and tremolos. A *trill* is the rapid alternation of two different notes; a *tremolo* is usually but not always the rapid reiteration of a single note or chord. Ask your children if these trills and tremolos sound like birds.

2. Another enjoyable activity is to discuss spring in general. How grand to be able to see the grass growing and the flowers blooming! What kind of sports will your pupils be starting?

You might have them bring baseball caps and bats to class if they are beginning to think about their own "spring training."

3. Do you know the song "Welcome Sweet Springtime"? It was made from Anton Rubinstein's *Melody in F*. Place Figure 60 on the board and play the opening melody.

Wel-come sweet spring - time...
F   E   F   F   E

Figure 60

4. The peacock is one of the most beautiful of birds. The "White Peacock" is a *virtuoso* piece for piano, which means that the pianist has to be very, very good to play it. You can show pictures of a peacock before or while you listen to the composition. You might also tell your students that Griffes died very young (he was 36), just as Mozart and Schubert did. If you can find an old peacock feather in your attic, you might bring it to class. Young children will giggle if you tickle their noses with it and then everyone will be in a good mood for listening to some beautiful impressionistic music. (Note: Griffes was strongly influenced by the French impressionist school.)

5. "Spring" from *The Four Seasons* by Vivaldi is a frequently played work and one your students should enjoy. Like Respighi's "Spring," it uses trills and tremolos to imitate birds. You might point out that Vivaldi was a contemporary of the great Johann Sebastian Bach (who was born on the first day of spring). You can also point out that Vivialdi's "Spring" was wirtten in the 18th Century while Respighi wrote his about 200 years later.

6. If you are really and truly sorry to see the winter go, you can listen to Wayne Barlow's *Rhapsody for Oboe,* also called "The Winter's Past." It is a good work to demonstrate the unique sound of the oboe (so that you don't have to use the hackneyed descriptions of the oboe's "nasal" sound). You might also use the composition to motivate a comparison of what you like and don't like about both winter and spring. Try a debate!

Japanese American Week

Grades: 2-8.

Materials: Picture of a *koto*—a Japanese string instrument; a Japanese songbook; a recording of Japanese music containing the *koto*.

Concepts:

1. Japanese American Week is usually celebrated at the end of March.
2. One of the most distinctive Japanese instruments is the *koto*, a string instrument played something like the *sitar*.

**Activities
&
Directions**

1. Background activities for this lesson can include finding Japan on the map or, with older students, discussing the tragedy of our treatment of Japanese Americans during World War II. The subject is controversial, but it is worth discussing. There are two television films that have dealt with this topic. Have you or your students ever seen them?

2. We all know the "sound" that immediately makes us think of Japanese music and Japan. But did you know that it is the instrument the *koto* that usually creates this sound? Chances are that a recording of Japanese traditional music will contain this instrument. The koto is derived from the Chinese ch'in, and its 13 strings are made of waxed silk, equal in length and thickness and tuned by movable bridges. It is usually about six feet long, nine inches wide and three inches high. It rests on

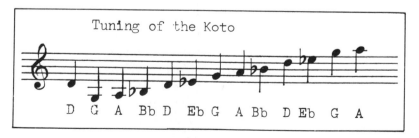

Figure 61

the floor with the right end raised by two small pegs. The player sits on the floor. It is usually tuned as shown in Figure 61.

COMPOSERS OF THE MONTH

The Little Train of the Caipira
(Heitor Villa-Lobos)
(March 5)

Grades: K-5.

Materials: Toy trains; recording of *The Little Train of the Caipira* (from *Bachianas Brasileiras No. 2*) by Heitor Villa-Lobos.

Concepts:

1. Villa-Lobos was a Brazilian composer who was born in Rio de Janeiro on March 5, 1887.
2. The Little Train starts slowly, gets faster and faster, and then slows down to a halt.
3. *The Little Train of the Caipira* is both a nationalistic piece and part of a tribute to the great German master Johann Sebastian Bach.

**Activities
&
Directions**

1. *The Little Train of the Caipira* has been used by many music teachers as an example of descriptive music. It is one of those compositions that is usually so well received that little has to be said about it. With younger children, all you might have to do is have them play with a set of trains and play the music. With older children, background and preparatory activities can include finding Rio de Janeiro on a map of Brazil and learning the names of the authentic percussion instruments from Brazil that create the effects of the Caipira train puffing and gasping, bumping, chugging, wheezing, and squeaking along:

   reco-reco (a notched wooden cylinder)
   chucalho (rattle with gourd seeds)
   ganza (metal tube filled with gravel)
   matraca (a ratchet)

2. Another enjoyable activity is to tell the story that this composition was inspired by a ride that Villa-Lobos took in 1931 on just such a noisy train, which was transporting berry pickers and farm laborers between villages in the Brazilian province of Sao Paolo ("Capipira" means "yokel" or "rustic"). Can the children say "caipira" or the original Indian word (of the Tupi Indians of Brazil) "curupira"?

Maurice of March
(March 7)

Grades: 4-8.

Materials: Recordings of Maurice Ravel's *Bolero* and *Rapsodie Espagnole;* map of Europe; slides or reproductions of impressionistic paintings.

Concepts:

1. Maurice Ravel (born March 7, 1875) was a French composer of the impressionist period.
2. The bolero is a Spanish dance and dance rhythm.

**Activities
&
Directions**

1. *Bolero* might very well be Ravel's best-known composition. Play a little of the beginning and then write the bolero rhythm on the board (see Figure 62). Since the rhythm is repeated throughout the composition, before long some of your students might be able to clap the rhythm. You might want to point out that in music a triplet is a group of three notes, as shown in Figure 62. Or you might point out that this rhythm

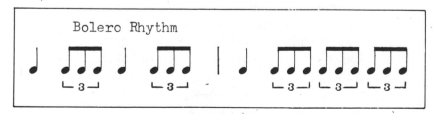

Figure 62

continues throughout the composition, the music getting louder and louder (which is called a *crescendo*).

2. Other activities can be to show how close Spain and France are on the map and to discuss how many French and Russian composers were inspired by Spanish rhythms (such as the bolero). *Bolero* and *Rapsodie Espagnole* were both inspired by Spanish music. Sing "Happy Birthday" to Ravel with some of your students playing the bolero rhythm. Try to identify the solo instruments as you listen to *Bolero*. Look at slides or reprints of impressionistic paintings. Draw the crescendo sign on the chalkboard (see Figure 63) and have your pupils practice drawing it.

The crescendo sign*

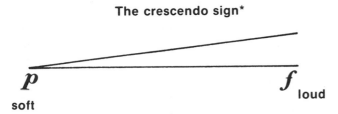

p   *f* loud

soft

***specific music determines how much louder one gets**

Figure 63

Happy Birthday Rimsky-Korsakov
(March 18)

Grades: K-4.

Materials: Honey; pictures or slides of bumble bees; map of Europe; recording of *Flight of the Bumble Bee* (piano or orchestra); piano.

Concepts:

1. Many great musicians have composed tunes that describe insects.

2. Compositions about insects often achieve their effects through *chromaticism*.

Activities
&
Directions

1. As background for listening to *Flight of the Bumble Bee,* discuss bumble bees and some of the activities they perform during the spring and summer months. You can show students pictures or slides, and you might even sweeten things up by eating some honey!

2. Young children love funny names. We bet that they will find the full name of Nicholas Andreievitch Rimsky-Korsakov funny! After some laughter, it will be easy to get them to sing "Happy Birthday" to Rimsky-Korsakov. Will they be able to guess what country he was born in? (Answer: Tikhvin, Russia on March 18, 1844.)

3. *Flight of the Bumble Bee* is used very often in television programs or movies made especially for children, so they will probably recognize the composition even if they don't know it's name. What they won't know is that the sound of the bumble bee in flight is achieved through use of *chromaticism*, which is moving by half steps or using flats and sharps. The word comes from the Greek "chromos," meaning color. You might demonstrate chromaticism by playing C, C♯, D, D♯ or E, E♭, D, D♭, C. If a piano is not available, resonator bells can be used.

4. You might want to mention that Rimsky-Korsakov wrote *Capriccio Espagnol,* adding him to the list of French and Russian composers inspired by Spanish music. Show how far away Russia is from Spain on a map.

Happy Birthday Johann Sebastian Bach
(March 21)

Grades: 4-8.

Materials: Chalk and chalkboard; any recording of the Swingle Singers performing Bach compositions, any recording containing Bach's Passacaglia and Fugue in C Minor, or a recording of any of the Brandenburg Concertos.

Concept: Bach was one of the greatest masters of "counterpoint" that ever lived. Counterpoint is a musical technique somewhat related to the round or canon. "Row, Row, Row Your Boat" and "Are You Sleeping?" are examples of the round or canon.

Activities & Directions

1. Place on the chalkboard:

HAPPY BIRTHDAY JOHANN SEBASTIAN BACH
(March 21, 1685)

Try to sing "Happy Birthday" as a round or canon. For practice, sing the round *Frere Jacques* or "Are You Sleeping" and explain that the delayed entry of a melody, as in this round, is one type of counterpoint that Bach used frequently. You might also listen to a Swingle Singers recording and ask the children to raise their hands when they hear a part that sounds like a round (or do the same with any of the *Brandenburg Concertos* or the Passacaglia and Fugue in C Minor). You might want to experiment with singing "Happy Birthday" in different ways, using "Happy Birthday Dear Johann" or "Happy Birthday Sebastian" or "Happy Birthday Dear Ba-ach." Note too, that Johann is German for John. It might be fun to relate this to "Are you sleeping . . . brother John. . . ?"

2. Related background activity can be to try to find Eisenach on a map of Germany. It is now in East Germany, and older students can discuss the political aspects of this. It might also be fun for the children to compute how old Bach would have been had he lived up until the American Revolution (he died in 1750).

Happy Birthday Modest Mussorgsky
(March 21)

Grades: K-5.

Materials: Pictures of eggs or a hen sitting on eggs; bells; crown cut from paper or cardboard; recording of "Ballet of the Unhatched Chicks" from *Pictures at an Exhibition;* recording of the "Coronation Scene" from *Boris Godunov.*

Concepts:

> 1. Modest Mussorgsky was a nationalistic composer born in Pskof (what is now Russia or the U.S.S.R.).
>
> 2. *Pictures at an Exhibition* is "program" or descriptive music; *Boris Godunov* is an opera.

**Activities
&
Directions**

> 1. On the chalkboard, write:
>
> HAPPY BIRTHDAY MODEST MUSSORGSKY
> (March 21, 1839)
> (Sometimes given as March 9, 1839)
>
> Ask the students if they can guess what country he was born in (you may have to read the name for younger students). Will they guess Russia? You might show how big Russia is on a map as a background activity.
>
> 2. In preparation for listening to "Ballet of the Unhatched Chicks," you can discuss chickens and how they are hatched. Students can bring in pictures of hens sitting on their nests of eggs (comic books often have such pictures). Mention that the chick has to break the egg in order to hatch. Then play the music and ask your pupils if they can tell where in the music the shell is being broken. They can raise their hands when they hear this. Tell the children that this is descriptive music.
>
> 3. Just listening to the "Coronation Scene" from Mussorgsky's nationalistic opera *Boris Godunov* can be dull for young children. But you can make it into a very exciting experience by having your pupils make and wear paper or cardboard crowns, creating your own coronation. Children love to play king and queen. Added excitement can be created by ringing bells when they are rung in the opera and discussing the fact that in the opera Boris goes insane.

**Happy Birthday Haydn
(March 31)**

Grades: K-5.

Materials: Toys (any); recordings of the *Toy* Symphony and Symphony

No. 94 in G (the *Surprise* Symphony), especially the "Andante" movement.

Concepts:

1. Haydn, an early classical composer, wrote 104 symphonies. It used to be quite fashionable to call him "Papa" Haydn, the "father of the symphony."
2. Haydn's last symphony has been nicknamed the *Toy* Symphony.

Activities
&
Directions

1. Listen to the "Andante" from Franz Joseph Haydn's 94th Symphony. Some of your pupils might discover that it sounds like "Twinkle Twinkle Little Star" and might even start singing along with the recording. (See Figure 64.) But will they be surprised by the loud chord Haydn used to try to make some of the ladies of the court jump? Record jacket "blurbs" often tell this story, so if your record library contains more than one version of this symphony, look for this story on one of them. This symphony was written in 1791 or 1792, and older students can discuss the fact that Franz Joseph Haydn, born March 31, 1732, was 44 years old at the time of the American Revolution and 57 at the start of the French Revolution.

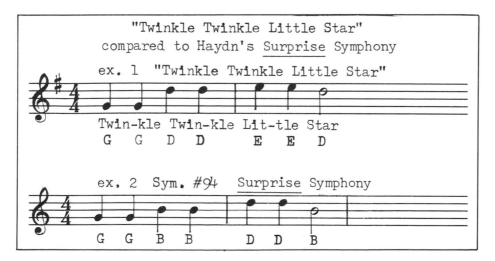

Figure 64

2. A particularly "fun" activity for younger children is to listen to Haydn's *Toy* Symphony while playing with any toys that might be appropriate. Listen for instruments that don't seem to be part of the regular orchestra.

3. An additional background activity can center around the fact that Haydn was born in Rohrau, Austria, and after he became a successful composer he worked for Prince Nicolaus II of the House of Esterhazy (of the Austro-Hungarian Empire).

8

APRIL

When you are teaching children, how can you not be happy in April? They are so cheerful and funny when playing the traditional April Fool's Day pranks on each other—and on you! And don't forget, children love to know that the teacher has a sense of humor, too. They may not be fooled by a prankish "you dropped something," but they sure will "be on your side," so to speak, when you want more mature behavior.

Musically, there is no shortage of topics for lessons this month—from Easter to Passover, World Health Day, Pan-American Day, and Arbor Day. And there are fringe benefits connected with these topics: chocolate bunnies, walks in the woods or a park, dancing to music to "keep in shape," and exciting Latin American rhythms.

Among the states that were admitted to the union in April are Maryland (the song about Maryland was originally about a tree, thus relating the song and the state, in a way, to Arbor Day) and Louisiana (birthplace of jazz and where they celebrate *Mardi Gras* or *Carnival*).

The famous conductor Leopold Stokowski (known by many children for his role in the Walt Disney classic *Fantasia*) was born on April 13. And the composer of the children's classic *Peter and the Wolf* was born on April 23.

Don't forget to capitalize on "April showers," the beautiful visions of "April in Paris," and the traditional joy brought by "April Love." Foliage and bulbs are already blooming—and pretty soon those April showers will bring May flowers! Enjoy it as the children do.

187

April

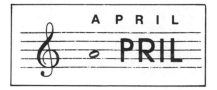

Figure 65

Grades: K-8.

Materials: Chalk and chalkboard or music flash cards.

Concept: Each letter of the alphabet can open up a world of music. April begins with A.

**Activities
&
Directions**

1. Place Figure 65 on the chalkboard or on music flashcards. Ask your students if they know what the music note in the figure is. If they tell you it is a whole note, be sure to tell them that this is correct but that it also has another name—A—and the note's full name is "A Whole Note." With younger students, we have successfully used the concept of a first name and a last name. If you use this approach, what you do is ask a child for his or her first name; e.g., Janet. Explain that this is like the A part of the note. Then ask for the second name; e.g., Smith. Explain that this is like the "Whole Note" part of the note. Therefore, Janet Smith is like "A Whole Note, and all notes have two names. You might give other examples such as "B Half Note" or "C Quarter Note."

2. As in previous months, ask your students to name performers, compositions, or composers whose names begin with A. List them on the chalkboard, and to those elicited from the students you might add musical terms such as *adagio* and *allegro* (which older pupils can look up in a music dictionary). You can also list the *Academic Festival Overture,* which Johannes Brahms composed in acknowledgment of the Ph.D. degree conferred on him by the University of Breslau in 1880 and which uses the

well-known song of rejoicing "Gaudeamus Igitur" (Wherefore let us rejoice). (See Figure 66.)

Figure 66

April Fool's Day

Grades: K-8.

Materials: Funny or comical music (such as *Facade* by William Walton, whose birthday was March 29); any songs about April such as "April Love" and "April Showers"; Gregorian chants.

Concepts:

1. April is the fourth month of the year according to the Gregorian calendar, but it was the second month of the Persian and Roman years.

2. April comes from the Latin *aperire* ("to open").

**Activities
&
Directions**

1. The custom of playing tricks may be a practice that survived as a residuum of pagan riotous festivals held at the vernal equinox (a great topic, by the way, for your astronomical geniuses). In France, a victim of such practical jokes was called an April fish (*poisson d'Avril*). In addition to playing the normal practical jokes (children *love* April Fool's Day), your children might want to listen to *Facade* by William Walton, whose birthday was last month. See if your children find it funny or discover the musical jokes that this composition contains.

2. Since April showers are like a joke of nature (how odd that it can be raining when the sun is shining), some music teachers play Al Jolson's rendition of "April Showers" around this time of the year.

3. You can use the topic of the spring or vernal equinox to discuss differences betwen lunar and solar calendars (or students can present reports). A related musical activity if you want to discuss Pope Gregory and the Gregorian calendar, is to expose your students to the sound of Gregorian chant. (It is *monodic* music, or *monody,* which means that it has a single melody sung in unison, with no countermelody and no harmony.)

April Love, April Showers, and April in Paris

Grades: K-8.

Materials: Recordings of "April in Paris," "April Showers," "Raindrops Keep Falling on my Head," "Singing in the Rain"; impressionistic pictures of Paris in the spring.

Concepts:

1. The month of April has inspired many songs such as "April in Paris."

2. The sun-showers that come in April have also inspired songs.

**Activities
&
Directions**

1. How interesting it is to be walking in the sun on a lovely, clear day only to find it raining a moment later. This is a typical example of something that adults get "all excited" about (Dear me, I forgot my umbrella!) but which children find an amusing and delightful experience. Ask your pupils if they have ever had this happen to them. Were they annoyed, or did they find it funny and fun? We bet they found it fun, especially the younger children. Act out such an occurrence and play a recording of "Singing in the Rain," "Raindrops Keep Falling on my Head," or the famous version of "April Showers" by Al Jolson.

2. Another enjoyable activity is to show pictures or slides of paintings of Paris in the spring by impressionist painters, playing a recording of "April in Paris" in the background. Have you ever been to Paris in the spring? Have any of your students? Can you describe your experiences, and is it as lovely as they say? If it is, tell your students about it—with enthusiasm!

3. We have successfully used the song "April Showers" to introduce the concept of the "accidental" (a sharp or flat not in the
key signature) to older pupils. You might want to try it, circling
the C sharp, as in Figure 67.

Though A - PRIL   SHOW--ERS

Figure 67

Israel in Egypt and Passover

Grades: 4-8.

Materials: World map or map of the Middle East; the oratorio *Israel in Egypt* by George Frederick Handel; the *Israel* Symphony by Ernest Bloch (or his work for cello and orchestra, *Schelomo*); unleavened bread (*Matzoth*).

Concepts:

1. Passover is a Jewish holiday commemorating the exodus of the Jews from Egypt and their safe flight across the Red Sea.
2. Unleavened bread, bread without yeast, is flat and dry and is called *matzoth.*
3. The sound of the cello.

**Activities
   &
Directions**

1. The term "Passover" is derived from the circumstance re-counted in the Old Testament in which an angel of the Lord, prior to striking down the first born male in every Egyptian household, instructed the Israelites to mark their dwellings with Lamb's blood so that the angel could identify them and thus "pass over" them. In the subsequent escape from Egypt and the flight into the desert, the term "Passover" became synonymous with passing over the Red Sea and the desert and

reaching the land of milk and honey 40 years later. *Matzoth* represents the unleavened bread that had to be eaten in the desert and is one of the traditional foods eaten at a *seder* (a Passover feast commemorating this holiday). Leonardo da Vinci's famous painting *The Last Supper* depicts a Passover *seder* (which can be shown to mature students). In the opera *La Boheme,* Act One, Scene One, Schaunard is painting a picture of Moses crossing the Red Sea.

2. Students can locate Egypt, Israel, and the Red Sea on the map, perhaps while munching on some *matzoth.* You might tell your students about, or play parts of, Handel's oratorio *Israel in Egypt* (a student report can be given on the oratorio). Or students can listen to the sound of the cello in Bloch's Hebraic rhapsody *Schelomo.*

Spring Sports

Grades: 3-8.

Materials: Chalk and chalkboard; paper; piano (not essential).

Concepts:

1. Musical creativity can include writing words to a song that are later set to music. The words to a song are called the lyrics.

2. Many baseball teams, and some basketball teams, have songs like college football teams do but there are few songs for golf or tennis.

**Activities
&
Directions**

1. Except for indoor tennis and miniature golf, one cannot play tennis and golf when there's snow on the ground. So we start playing golf and tennis in the spring. But why aren't there any golf and tennis songs? Since there are none (that we know of), perhaps you and your class can write one. If you can, what a racket. We suggest "Tee for Two" or something like that. You might *net* some good results! Call it "Net-Work" if you can't be *punnier* than we are. Oh yes—and have a ball! After you get a good *set* of lyrics, try to have it *set* to music (a professional

musician or the high school music teacher can do this). By the way, lots of *love,* because tennis is a *love*-ly game.

2. Many music teachers have found that a fistfull of notes played on a piano can represent hitting a tennis ball or teeing off. The sound is not quite the same, but it's a fair musical representation. A *glissando* can represent the swing right before one hits the tennis or golf ball. (Use the thumb nail for a *glissando.* The inverted thumb moves up or down the notes on the piano.)

Start of the Baseball Season

Grades: K-8.

Materials: None or baseball uniforms, caps, bats, and so on.

Concept: The baseball season starts in April. Many baseball teams have songs that are associated with them.

**Activities
&
Directions**

1. If you have not yet sung "Take Me Out to the Ballgame" this year, there is no better time than now. (See page 37.)

2. Your students may know songs that are associated with their favorite baseball team, sometimes through the radio station that broadcasts the games. Why not ask them (your students) to whistle one of these. This activity would probably be more fun if done in full baseball attire, but it can be done without any "props."

World Health Day
(April 7)

Grades: K-8

Materials: Any dance music; recording of, or words and music for, the song "Bicycle Built for Two"; recording of the type of music played at skating rinks; hiking music such as "Valderi" (The Happy Wanderer).

Concepts:

1. Dancing is one way of keeping physically fit; hiking, skating, and bicycle riding are others.
2. Dance music can be fast or slow depending upon the type of dance.
3. Songs have been written about hiking, skating, and riding bicycles.

Activities
&
Directions

1. In addition to proper diet and regular checkups and care by well-trained physicians, exercise is essential for proper health. Dancing is one of the many good exercises. One cannot think of dancing without thinking of music. You can discuss this fact with your students and emphasize the role music plays in all kinds of dances. Then, do some dancing in class. Have fun keeping fit!
2. While there may not be many bicycles built for two anymore, "Bicycle Built for Two" is the most famous song about bicycling that we know. The song can be sung or listened to on recording, followed by a discussion of how good an exercise riding a bicycle is. (See page 168.)
3. Hiking is another way of keeping fit and staying healthy. The best-known song about hiking is "Valderi" (The Happy Wanderer). (See page 29.)

> "I love to go a-wandering
> Along the mountain track
> And as I go, I love to sing
> My knapsack on my back
>   Valderi   Valdera
>   Valderi   Valdera-ha-ha-ha-ha-ha-ha"

Taping the Tap and Birds of Spring

Grades: 4-8.

Materials: Reel-to-reel or cassette tape recorder; blank cassette cartridges or reel of magnetic tape.

Concepts:

1. Electronic music can be created without using a synthesizer.

2. A simple water faucet can be used to obtain electronic sounds that sound similar to bird calls.

Activities
&
Directions

1. The sounds of birds are a familiar sound of spring. You may have heard your students imitate bird calls from time to time, but did you know that you can create bird-call sounds using a tape recorder? One way to do this is to tape the sound of a dripping water faucet at a slow speed and then play it back at a higher speed. Try it several times at home. Then, if the results are fairly good, play the resulting tape for your class. We suggest challenging them to do better (and they probably will!). Either a cassette recorder or a reel-to-reel tape recorder can be used.

2. Another enjoyable activity is to tape actual bird calls. Many music teachers have done this. Then, interesting electronic sounds can be obtained by either slowing down or speeding up the tape. We've had great success with this approach, and it calls for exciting walks through the woods, a city park, or a bird sanctuary.

3. Speaking of the "spring sound" of birds, more and more popular recordings have been using bird calls and other *musique concrète* (natural sounds not created by an instrument). Can your pupils make a list of recordings that start off with bird sounds? You'll be surprised by the list they come up with!

Peter Cottontail

Grades: K-2.

Materials: Assorted tennis balls, basketballs, small rubber balls; chocolate bunnies; cotton or crepe paper.

Concept: Rhythmic movement is an important preparatory experience to learning about accent and meter in music.

**Activities
     &
Directions**

1. Prior to this lesson, you and your students can spend some time making "tails" out of cotton or crepe paper. Of course, if you want to make the big rabbit ears, that's all right, too. Anything to make the lesson fun . . . even a full bunny costume.

2. Here's our "Peter Principle": children need some basic rhythmic movement, both for fun and to establish a sense of pulse or beat. A good way to do this, around Easter time, is to have the children bounce up and down like bunnies. They can bounce and count ONE two, ONE two, ONE two or ONE two three, ONE two three, ONE two three or ONE two three four, ONE two three four.

3. Balls (tennis, basketball, and so on) can also be used to develop this rhythmic impulse and a feeling for grouping beats. Chocolate bunnies can provide an incentive to learning, as well as having fun. If students learn that ONE two, ONE two means two beats in a measure, they get a chocolate bunny.

Easter Parade

Grades: K-5.

Materials: Record player; recording or music for the song "Easter Parade"; Easter bonnets, chocolate bunnies, Easter eggs, toy bunnies.

Concepts:

1. There is no formal "Easter Parade," but it is traditional to buy and show-off new clothing for Easter.

2. Bunnies (baby rabbits) and eggs represent fertility and life, which makes them symbolic of spring and Easter.

**Activities
     &
Directions**

1. The song "Easter Parade" referred not to a real parade but to how it has become a tradition to "parade" around in new Easter clothing, such as the "Easter bonnet" referred to in the

song. However, you can capitalize on this idea and have a miniature parade in your class! Tell your students in advance to think about what kind of clothing they will wear. Ask them to think about what kind of floats (toy and chocolate bunnies?) they will prepare. Spend a few days, perhaps, making floats that you can use. When you have your "parade," you might have both beautiful bonnets and delicious floats!

2. When you have your parade in class, either singing the song "Easter Parade" or marching to a recording of it, you might also introduce the concept of a march being in 4/4 meter (four beats in a measure) or, sometimes, two beats in a measure. Explain to the pupils that as you march, you count: ONE two three four, ONE two three four or ONE two, ONE two, ONE two, ONE two. Explain that four beats in a measure or a grouping of four beats is called 4/4 *meter* or a *time signature* of 4/4. Explain that two beats in a measure or grouping beats by twos is called 2/4 meter or a time signature of 2/4.

3. As background for this lesson, you might also discuss the meaning of bunnies and eggs and why they have remained a tradition of the Easter holiday (they are symbols of fertility and life).

What Did You Do on Your Easter Vacation?

Grades: 2-8.

Materials: Chalk and chalkboard; leftover Easter eggs.

Concepts:

1. Music plays an important role in almost every holiday season.
2. Many Easter songs have to do with the clothing one wears, Easter bunnies and eggs, and the festive as well as religious aspects of Easter.

Activities & Directions

1. Ask your students what they did on their Easter vacations and list some of these activities on the chalkboard. You might discuss things one does around Easter time and some of the songs about these activities (such as "Easter Parade" and "Peter Cot-

tontail"). Can any of your students sing an Easter song? Can anyone write out the words? They can be religious as well as secular, and you can discuss going to church and the Easter hymns that are sung.

2. Discussion of Easter vacation activities can include the spring sports that the children begin to play, and you can sing "Take Me Out to the Ballgame."

3. We have had fun with leftover Easter eggs. Here's an activity your students should get a kick out of. Place Figure 68 on the chalkboard, drawing the staff wide enough for the Easter eggs to fit in the spaces left for them; i.e., the eggs can be placed right over the egg-shaped notes that are on the staff. It is interesting to note that EGG is one of the words most frequently used when the game of making up words using only the musical alphabet of A B C D E F G is played.

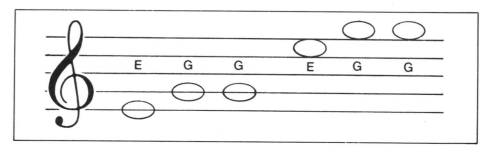

Figure 68

Pan-American Day
(April 14)

Grades: K-8.

Materials: Recorded music of Latin America (the most popular, such as Mexican, Brazilian, and Argentine, or the less well-known, such as that of Chile and Equador); map of South and Central America; colorful dress of Latin American countries; pictures of Latin American instruments; recordings by Yma Sumac.

Concepts:

1. Many South American rhythms and dances have been used by American dance orchestras (the tango, rhumba, bolero, samba, and so on).

2. Publications of the Pan-American Union are in three languages: English, Spanish, and Portuguese.

Activities & Directions

1. The Pan-American Union was established on April 14, 1890, in accordance with a resolution adopted by the First International Conference of American States, for the purpose of promoting peace, friendship, and commerce among member republics. Since it was established in 1890, you might want to play some "Gay '90's" music along with the Latin American dances you've chosen.

2. Latin American music is exciting, but you can add even more flair by obtaining or making colorful attire to go with the appropriate music. We've all seen pictures of Rudolph Valentino, so we can envision the "proper" way to dress when doing the tango. Similarly, older students can do research regarding the native dress of some of the South American countries, some of which have Indian influences such as in Peru. (We have found that the recordings of Yma Sumac are very well received by students of all ages.)

3. Can you teach your pupils how to do the rhumba or the bossa nova? If you can, this lesson should appeal to you. If not, you can listen to the music with your students and point out simple facts such as what the dance is and which country the music comes from.

The Firebird
(April 15)

Grades: 1-5.

Materials: Recording of *The Firebird* by Igor Stravinsky (the suite made from the ballet).

Concepts:

1. Igor Stravinsky was a very famous 20th Century composer.
2. *The Firebird* was originally a ballet, and some of the most exciting parts of the ballet were made into a suite.
3. In a ballet, men and women dance to music.

**Activities
&
Directions**

1. In preparation for listening to *The Firebird* suite, we've had great success with the following approach. Ask your pupils to name words with fire in them. Among the most frequently mentioned, which you can list on the chalkboard, are:

firefly	fire engine
fireboat	fire insurance
fireman	fire extinguisher
fire escape	fire department
Fire Island	fire place
firestone	fire alarm

    Then you can discuss these words and concepts. But have any of your students ever heard of a firebird? Probably not, because it is an aspect of Russian folklore, not American folklore. But we bet you can produce a lively discussion by asking your pupils to use their imaginations to try to describe or draw one.

2. Most record jackets contain the story of *The Firebird,* Igor Stravinsky's ballet, which was first performed in Paris on June 25, 1910, and in New York at the Metropolitan Opera House on April 15, 1916. It was commissioned by the great choreographer, Diaghilev and, in French, was called *L'Oiseau de Feu.* You might provide additional explanation by telling your class that Stravinsky later extracted some of the best-liked parts of the ballet and made it into a *suite* (which, originally, in the 16th century, was a collection or group of dance tunes).

Revere's Ride and the Pony Express

Grades: 3-7.

Materials: Any "horsey" music, from the traditional opening race track trumpet fanfare to the Schumann classic that was made into a popular song entitled "Wild Horses," the fugue from *Guys and Dolls* (which starts out "I got the horse right here, his name is Paul Revere. . . ."), the part of the *William Tell* Overture that was used as the Lone Ranger music, the Schubert classic *Erlkonig* (which depicts a desparate ride with a sick child), and the portion of the *1812 Overture* that depicts the retreating Napoleonic army.

Concepts:

1. In April 1775, Paul Revere made his famous ride to warn the continental army that the British were coming.

2. In April 1860, the first pony express delivery went out.

3. There are many different types and styles of music that make us think of, or are associated with, horses.

**Activities
&
Directions**

1. "Listen my children and you shall hear of the midnight ride of Paul Revere. . . ." is the opening line of a poem that many students used to have to memorize. Although memorization is not in fashion, why not use this poem to teach your students about the beginning of the American Revolution? Use some "horsey" music before, during, or after this lesson.

2. If you are dealing with the period right before the Civil War, you might discuss the pony express. As with Paul Revere's ride, choose whatever music you are able to obtain. Some music teachers have tried different music with the same idea, such as discussing the pony express and then putting on the *1812 Overture,* talking about it some more and playing Schubert's *Erlkonig,* and so on. (See page 137, #2.)

3. With young children, a simple question is: "In the fugue from *Guys and Dolls,* why was the horse's name Paul Revere?" (Answer: because it rhymes with "right here.") (See page 78.)

4. Can any of your pupil's make up a tune to "Listen my children and you shall hear of the midnight ride of Paul Revere. . . ."?

Another Original State
(April 28)

Grades: 2-8.

Materials: Map of the United States; recording of "Oh Maryland My Maryland" (Lindenbaum); chalkboard or music flashcards; the "Star Spangled Banner."

Concepts:

1. Dotted eighth note and sixteenth note.

2. 3/4 meter and time signature.

**Activities
&
Directions**

1. Background discussion for this lesson can include facts such as the state being named by Lord Baltimore in honor of Henrietta Maria, Queen of Charles I (King of England). Maryland was admitted to the Union on April 28, 1788. A famous railroad (for train collectors) is the Baltimore and Ohio Railroad, and one of our nation's finest medical schools, The Johns Hopkins University's medical college, is located in Maryland. The U.S. Naval Academy is located at Annapolis, Maryland. And the famous Potomac River has Indian-named "relatives" in the Pocomoke and Nanticoke Rivers, which are also in the state of Maryland.

2. The dotted eighth and sixteenth note pair (see below), used in

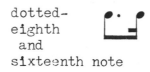

both our national anthem and "Oh Maryland My Maryland," can be introduced with the story that during the 1812 War, in September 1814, Fort McHenry in Baltimore withstood a severe bombardment by the British Fleet, and in the course of this battle, Francis Scott Key wrote the "Star Spangled Banner." Since forests figure prominently in the economy of Maryland, you might also point out that "Oh Maryland My Maryland" was originally a song about a Lindenbaum tree. It is also fun to note that the "Star Spangled Banner" has the exact same

Figure 69

rhythmic beginning as "Happy Birthday" (although the melody is different). Try clapping the opening rhythm of the two songs. Now place Figure 69 on the board and point out the dotted eighth and sixteenth note pairs. Have pupils circle them.

Arbor Day
(April 29)

Grades: K-8.

Materials: The poem and song "Trees"; pictures of trees; seedlings for planting.

Concepts:

1. Some poems have been set to music. When a poem is set to music it is called an *art song*.
2. Arbor Day is an annual tree-planting day.

**Activities
&
Directions**

1. In the United States, Arbor Day is an annual tree-planting day for the beautification of towns or forestation of empty lands. It is a legal holiday in some states. Among the Arbor Day activities that many teachers engage in with their classes are:

    (a) Planting trees.
    (b) Visiting an arboretum, which is a botanical garden in which trees constitute the principal objects of study.
    (c) Looking at pictures of trees to learn the names of the wide variety of trees that grow in this country.

   Are you lucky enough to live anywhere near the world famous California redwoods, the beautiful Green Mountains of Vermont, or the White Mountains of New Hampshire? Can you *smell* a pine tree when someone says the word? Have you seen acorns fall from oak trees? There is so much to talk about for Arbor Day!

2. "I think that I shall never see, a poem as lovely as a tree. . . ." Are there any children who have never heard this poem? If

your pupils have not, why not expose them to this lovely verse? You can recite the poem, sing the song, or listen to a recording of the song. Arbor Day is a perfect time to use this work.

Lovely Louisiana
(April 30)

Grades: K-8.

Matrials: Pictures of birds indigenous to Louisiana (such as the duck, wild goose, coot, snipe, rail, gallinule, woodcock, quail, wild turkey, and deer); books and other materials about the Creole culture; recordings of Dixeland jazz ("When the Saints Go Marching In" or "Basin Street Blues"); pictures of Louis "Satchmo" Armstrong; pictures of Baton Rouge or New Orleans; map of the United States.

Concepts:

1. New Orleans has been called the birthplace of jazz. New Orleans is one of the places in the U.S. where you can see a real Carnival.

2. Jazz originated in the United States.

Activities
&
Directions

1. A lesson on "Lovely Louisiana" is bound to be successful! How can children not be "turned on" by pictures of "Satchmo," as Louis Armstrong, who for three decades was our best goodwill ambassador, was nicknamed? (Do any of your students have nicknames like that? Why not discuss them? Then listen to some of Louis Armstrong's most famous recordings, such as "When the Saints Go Marching In.") And no state has a greater variety or abundance of game birds. How can children not be "turned on" by pictures of the wild turkey or the wild goose (Do you know the famous recording by Frankie Lane "My heart goes where the wild goose goes. . . ."?).

2. Older students can do reports on the Creole culture that gave birth to jazz or locate Baton Rouge and New Orleans on the map. You can provide information about the Louisiana Purchase in 1803 and how France needed money at the time,

resulting in the largest single acquisition of land in the history of the United States. Louisiana was admitted as a state on April 30, 1812. You might even go into earlier history and tell students about Louisiana being discovered in 1682 by LaSalle and being named after King Louis XIV.

3. Younger students can "stage" the stereotyped but still fascinating funeral procession that one often sees in movies, with slow, sad music at first that later breaks out into Dixieland jazz. Or they can stage a miniature Carnival with colorful costumes! They might also be interested to learn that the steamboat helped make the state capital, Baton Rouge, the great port city it is.

COMPOSERS OF THE MONTH

"Stokey" and Fantasia:
Happy Birthday Leopold Stokowski
(April 13)

Grades: K-8.

Materials: The film *Fantasia* (if you can obtain it); chalk and chalkboard; any recording of the Bach-Stokowski arrangements (Bach works arranged for orchestra by Leopold Stokowski), such as his arrangement of the Toccata and Fugue in D Minor; any recording of Leopold Stokowski conducting the Philadelphia Orchestra or the American Symphony Orchestra (which he organized when he was in his late 70's!).

Concepts:

1. Leopold Stokowski was a living legend, conducting and arranging on into his 95th year!
2. Many children became familiar with "Stokey," as he was affectionately known, through his appearance in the Walt Disney classic *Fantasia*.

Activities
&
Directions

1. Stokowski was fascinated with J.S. Bach's compositions, and he rearranged many of them for modern orchestra. Many of

these orchestral transcriptions are musical masterpieces, such as the Bach-Stokowski Toccata and Fugue in D Minor. You might explain that such hyphenated "credits" indicate that the work was originally composed by the first person but later arranged or re-arranged by the second person.

2. If you are lucky enough to hear about a theater that is showing *Fantasia,* the Walt Disney film classic, schedule a trip to see it with your class. It is a brilliant film, and it includes a filmed segment of the fairly young Leopold Stokowski conducting the famed Philadelphia Orchestra. Perhaps your school can rent the film. One of the works that the film includes is Stravinsky's classic *Le Sacre du Printemps* (The Rite of Spring). How appropriate for April!

3. Place on the chalkboard:

HAPPY BIRTHDAY STOKEY
(April 13, 1882)

Younger children will be amused by the nickname "Stokey." Older children can be taught the proper pronunciation: LEE-O-POLD STO-KOF-SKEE.

Happy Birthday Prokofiev
(April 23)

Grades: K-8.

Materials: Recordings of Prokofiev's *Peter and the Wolf* and his suite from the ballet *Cinderella;* chalk and chalkboard; map of Europe.

Concepts:

1. Fairy tales and children's stories are often set to music.
2. Serge Prokofiev was a Russian composer. He is particularly known by school children because of his *Peter and the Wolf* (a musical fairy tale in which every character is portrayed by a musical instrument).

Activities
&
Directions

1. Place on the chalkboard:

HAPPY BIRTHDAY SERGE PROKOFIEV
(April 23, 1891)

You might discuss the fact that any day can be the birthday of a famous composer. Another background activity can be to compute how many years after Prokofiev's birth the United States entered World War II. (Answer: 50 years.) Ask students to guess where Prokofiev was born (Sontsovka, Russia) or to find the country of his birth on the map.

2. An amusing way to introduce *Peter and the Wolf* is to ask students if the name Peter refers to Peter Cottontail! It sounds plausible, and some children will probably say yes. But then you can tell them that this Peter is a boy, not a rabbit. Most recordings discuss the story, so we needn't go into it here. We'll only say that the recording has delighted children ever since it was written in 1936. We're sure you and your students will enjoy it. See if you can recognize the bassoon as Peter's grandfather, the French horns as the wolf, and the sounds of the clarinet and the flute.

3. Older children might prefer the Cinderella story to *Peter and the Wolf*. The Cinderella story is well known. It might be interesting to note your pupils' reactions to the suite from Prokofiev's ballet. Be sure to listen for the waltz and point out that a waltz is in 3/4 meter.

Happy Birthday Charlie Chaplin

Grades: K-5.

Materials: Chalk and chalkboard; "Eternally," the theme from *Limelight*.

Concepts:

1. Charlie Chaplin (Charles Spencer Chaplin) was one of the all-time greats of silent movies as a beloved comedian.

2. The theme from *Limelight*, "Eternally," is a waltz in 3/4 time or meter.

Activities & Directions

1. Are there any students in your class who have never seen excerpts of Charlie Chaplin movies? We doubt it, but if there are any, why not be a sport and imitate his funny way of walking! Use an umbrella, of course, and a derby or bowler hat. What a treat it would be if your school or school district has a collection of Charlie Chaplin films on video-tape. Or perhaps some

museum or movie theater is going to schedule a Charlie Chaplin film festival. We suggest this as a marvelous trip.

2. Much later in life (he was born in 1889), Charlie Chaplin started directing and producing films. He even wrote the theme for one. It is "Eternally," from his film *Limelight,* and it is a beautiful waltz. (See Figure 70.) If you have not yet taught the concept that a waltz is in 3/4 meter or time (three beats in a measure), here is your chance!

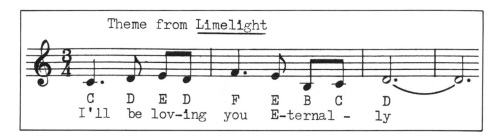

Figure 70

9

MAY

Like March, May is a truly musical month. From the Charleston May Festival to Be Kind to Animals Week, Mother's Day, American Indian Day, and United Nations Day, there is a wealth of musical material to draw upon. You can dance the Charleston and teach about the "roaring twenties" (the "flappers," bootleggers, and so on). You can include pop "classics" such as "How Much Is That Doggie in the Window," "Mule Train," "We are Siamese if You Please," and "Donkey Serenade." Even "Mary Had a Little Lamb" can be included. Who can forget George Jessel singing "My Mother's Eyes"? And what children fail to respond to American Indian music?

Some of the most popular *classical* composers were born in May: Johannes Brahms, Peter Ilyitch Tchaikovsky, Sir Arthur Sullivan, William Grant-Still. Their international character makes for a marvelous tie-in with United Nations Day (or May Day or United Nations Month). William Grant-Still's *Afro-American Symphony* involves two continents. Sullivan's music has been as popular in America as it has been in England. Brahms's birthplace, Hamburg, was where the hamburger originated, but it has been America where the hamburger developed its international character.

May saw Minnesota, South Carolina, Rhode Island, and Wisconsin admitted as states. Wisconsin is world famous for its cheese, of course, as well as the "On Wisconsin" melody that many football fans know. The 3M Corporation has made Minnesota world famous, and many children know about tiny Rhode Island being our smallest state.

Enjoy your Maypole dances, the Charleston, and the May flowers. Most of all, make May a musical month.

May

Figure 71

Grades: K-8.

Materials: Chalk and chalkboard or music flash cards.

Concept: Each letter of the alphabet can open up a world of music. May begins with M, but rhymes with A.

**Activities
&
Directions**

1. Place Figure 71 on the chalkboard or on music flash cards. Ask your students if they know what the musical note in the figure is. From second grade on up, most students should know the correct answer, but they may not. Try saying, "The note rhymes with May," but don't tell them that it is the first letter in the alphabet (although you can use that approach if you are teaching children with perceptual problems or some retardation). If you haven't used similar lessons for other months, turn to April's first lesson. It explains that the note is a whole note as well as being a musical "A."

2. As in previous months, ask your students to name performers, compositions, or composers whose names begin with M. List them on the chalkboard, and to those elicited from the students, you might add Mozart and Monteverdi (see the first lesson in the March chapter for additional examples). You might also use the last letter of May, Y, and list Yang Ch'in (a Chinese dulcimer), "Yankee Doodle" (the song), and *Yeomen of the Guard* (an operetta written by Sir Arthur Sullivan, who was born on May 13 of this month).

Charleston May Festival
(First Week in May)

Grades: 3-8.

Materials: Classical music of your choice.

Concepts:

1. May music festivals are popular in this country.
2. The Charleston May Festival is a biennial festival of classical music, as is the Chattanooga May Music Festival.

**Activities
&
Directions**

1. Why not have a May music festival in your classroom, in the schoolyard, or on your school lawn. You can use the classical music of your choice. You might want to use compositions that have been inspired by May (such as two piano compositions by Sir Arnold Bax *May Night in Ukraine* and *On a May Evening*).

2. Charleston (West Virginia) and Chattanooga (Tennessee) are among the states that have May music festivals. A background activity for this lesson might be locating these cities and their states. If you want to introduce some lighter music, there is a song entitled "Chattanooga Choo-Choo" ("Pardon me boys, this is the Chattanooga Choo Choo, track twenty-nine. . . .").

Be Kind to Animals Week

Grades: K-6.

Materials: Recordings of songs such as "How Much Is That Doggie in the Window?" "We Are Siamese if You Please," "Mary Had a Little Lamb," "Mule Train," "Donkey Serenade," "Smokey the Bear," and "Teddy Bear's Picnic"; literature from the Humane Society or the American Society for the Prevention of Cruelty to Animals; pictures of animals; toy animals; Melode Bells.

Concepts:

1. Animals are sometimes "man's best friend"; they also provide us with fur, milk, and so on.

2. There are many songs about animals.

**Activities
&
Directions**

1. Next to lessons about ecology, this is one of the lessons we most like to give. Doesn't just the thought of a beloved pet make you smile or feel good all over? Your students will love to place toy animals or pictures of animals all over the room. Then you can listen to any or all of the suggested songs. Younger students can point to the animals that are mentioned.

2. Another way to structure this lesson is to invite a guest from the Humane Society or the American Society for the Prevention of Cruelty to Animals. There is considerable difference of opinion between these two groups, so if you have speakers from both there might be some interesting, heated discussion.

3. Songs about animals are often easy to play, possibly because they are designed to appeal to children. Have you ever played "Mary Had a Little Lamb" on the Melode Bells? (See Figure 72.)

Figure 72

**Mother's Day
(Second Sunday in May)**

Grades: K-4.

Materials: Construction paper, crayons, paint, and other materials for making Mother's Day cards; songs such as "My Mom," "My

Mother's Wedding Day" from the Broadway musical *Briga-doon,* and "My Mother's Eyes"; Melode Bells.

Concepts:

1. On Mother's Day, children and husbands give or make cards for the mother of the family.

2. Songs have been written about and inspired by mothers.

3. A quarter rest (in common time) receives one beat.

Activities
&
Directions

1. Place Figure 73 on the chalkboard and explain that it is the beginning of a song made famous by George Jessel called "My Mother's Eyes." Circle the quarter rest as we have done. You might ask your pupils what the quarter rest looks like to them (a typical answer is like a lightning bolt). Can you rest on the first beat of these measures and hum the other notes? We've indicated the letter names so you can teach it to your students on the resonator or Melode Bells if you want to.

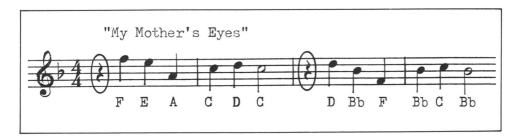

Figure 73

2. Another enjoyable activity is for the children to make cards for their mothers from construction paper. Children always love this. As background "listening music" you can play any songs based on or inspired by Mother's Day.

3. "My Mammy" is a song about a substitute mother. Some third and fourth graders might be mature enough to discuss this topic. (Have they ever heard Al Jolson?)

Scotch Tape Anyone?
(May 11)

Grades: 3-8.

Materials: Scotch tape or any other 3M Corporation products; pictures of Minneapolis; pictures of mines in Minnesota; miners' hats; recording of the song "Minnesota March On" (optional).

Concepts:

1. Since Fort Sumpter was fired on in April of 1861, Minnesota became a state almost exactly three years before the start of the Civil War (on May 11, 1858).
2. The song "Minnesota March On" is in 6/8 meter.
3. Minnesota is a state rich in natural resources.

**Activities
&
Directions**

1. Fun background activities can include displaying scotch tape or any other products manufactured by the Minnesota Mining and Manufacturing Corp., looking at pictures of Minneapolis or the vast mines in Minnesota, and putting on hard hats and other mining gear. You might also discuss the serious side of mining and the extreme dangers involved.

2. If you tell your students that Minnesota became a state three years before the outbreak of the Civil War, will they know the correct date? If they are above the fifth grade they should! Younger students can solve the simple problem: $1861 - 3 =$ ____?

3. "Minnesota March On" is the Minnesota University football

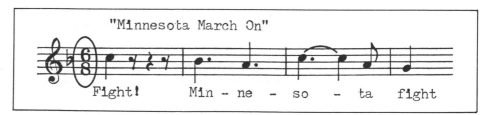

Figure 74

fight song. It is a lively tune in 6/8 meter. If you know the song or can obtain a recording of it, you can use it to introduce the concept of 6/8 meter. We've circled the 6/8 time signature, and you can, too. (See Figure 74.) You can also circle the flat sign and the rests if you want to review these symbols.

American Indian Day

Grades: K-8.

Materials: Reproductions of paintings such as "Life Among the Plains Indians" by A. A. Jackson; United States map; Indian blankets, sandals, dolls, and other objects made by American Indians; the type of Indian "outfit" often sold in children's toy stores; recording of Edward MacDowell's Second Suite, subtitled the "Indian" Suite, or his piano solo entitled *Indian Idyl* (Op. 62, No. 6).

Concepts:

1. Most of what we have come to think of as Indian music has come from Hollywood and is a European conception.
2. Real American Indian music has been studied by people known as ethno-musicologists (musicologists who specialize in studying music of a specific culture).

Activities & Directions

1. Edward MacDowell's Second Suite, Op. 48, uses authentic North American Indian melodies and was one of the first compositions to present native American folksong elements in artistic music. (Many of the compositions that "signal" the stereotyped Indian raid on the covered wagon have no relationship to the authentic music of the indigenous American peoples.) Listen to the five movements and see if you can hear the Indian melodies. The movements are: (1) *Legend,* (2) *Lovesong,* (3) *In War Time,* (4) *Dirge,* and (5) *Village Festival.*
2. Oddly enough, one year before the publication of MacDowell's "Indian Suite" in 1897, the young Prokofiev, at the age of *five,*

improvised a composition that he called *Indian Gallup.* It was written down by his mother. This was in 1896, which shows that the world was beginning to be responsive to and influenced by American Indian music. (Note: this was an even 20 years before the first "American Indian Day," which might make an interesting mathematical exercise for your pupils.) You can also discuss the phenomenon of a five-year-old child improvising at the piano.

3. You might want to discuss the job of the ethno-musicologist. If you see a puzzled look in your pupils' eyes, you might use the joke "Musicology is what a musicologist does!" Then explain that some ethno-musicologists collect, analyze, and classify American Indian song literature. For example, Figure 75 shows two measures of a Shawnee Hunting Dance. If you can manage to play this segment, a good time can be had by all by setting up a tepee or having younger pupils put on their Indian outfits or Indian sandals. After all, you don't need to do much to get young children to play Indian! Why not look at pictures, also, such as "Life Among the Plains Indians" by A. A. Jackson.

"Shawnee Hunting Dance" excerpt

Figure 75

4. Having used music as a motivation, some teachers begin to delve into the more serious ramifications of the Indian situation in our country. Start off with simple facts such as Columbus calling the American aborigines "Indians" because he thought he had sailed around the world and reached India. Using a map, list cities, states, rivers, bays, lakes, and so on that have Indian names (try for 200!). Students can present reports on "Indian Territory" or "Indian Reservations." Discuss the way we take the name Miami for granted and forget that the Miami were a tribe or confederacy of tribes closely allied with the Wea and Piankashaw tribes who were traditionally hostile to the Iroquois. After discussing corn, canoes, Navaho blankets, the Indian game "Hunt the Button" (which you can play),

or the fact that Indians raised corn, tobacco, peanuts, beans, squash, pumpkins, sunflowers, gourds, and cotton, you might be ready to get into some controversial material. For example: It wasn't until June 2, 1924 that Congress declared that all Indians born within the territorial limits of the United States are automatically citizens. It wasn't until 1934 that Congress passed the Indian Reorganization Act, which has been called the Indian's *Magna Charta,* permitting tribes to govern their own members, incorporate, obtain Federal loans, and so on. Finally, in simple terms, it can be explained that the indigenous Americans or aboriginal peoples had as many differences as similarities—linguistically, culturally, and anatomically. The MacDowell or other Indian pieces can be played softly in the background of such a discussion.

United Nations Month

Grades: K-8.

Materials: Recordings of Alan Hovhanness' Symphony No. 11 "All Men Are Brothers," Beethoven's Ninth or Choral Symphony, the song "It's a Small World"; pictures of all kinds of people from all over the world.

Concepts:

1. The United Nations' representatives and certain agencies of the U.N. try to help people learn to live without war and deal with the world problems of hunger, poor health, and disasters created by nature.

2. The United Nations is a place where people from all over the world gather to discuss their differences as well as their similarities.

Activities & Directions

1. At different times during the year, we celebrate "Brotherhood Week" and "United Nations Day." We should probably engage in some discussion of this theme *every* day! We shouldn't be able to get enough of it! Sometimes May is considered United Nations Month, perhaps because of May Day celebrations held

in various parts of the world. We've had great success playing music from all over the world to compare the different sounds. You can choose anything, and we have not listed specific suggestions above. The idea is simply to expose children to music that is quite different from what we are used to hearing.

2. Can your class sing "It's a Small World"? (See Figure 76.) After the song, some teachers discuss the ethnic backgrounds of the students in the class and the school community. You might also discuss how we know much more about foods and clothing of different peoples in the world than we used to.

It's a small world af-ter all
F   F   A   F   G   G   G

Figure 76

3. Many music teachers use the Symphony No. 11 ("All Men Are Brothers") by Alan Hovhannes, because the title is so very appropriate. Hovhannes is a 20th Century composer whose music is exciting but often dissonant. You might want to compare this with Beethoven's Ninth Symphony ("The Choral").

4. The last movement of Beethoven's Ninth Symphony uses the famous poem "Ode to Joy" by the German poet Schiller. Before you listen to it, one enjoyable activity might be writing poems about brotherhood, peace, and love. Compare your students' poems with the lines from Schiller's poem:

> "Let thy magic bring together
> All whom earthborn laws divide
> All mankind shall be as brothers
> Where thy gentle wings abide"

The music from Beethoven's Ninth Symphony is also used by many music teachers because it is easy to play (see Figure 77). Noting that it starts on F♯, you can try playing it on the piano or resonator bells. The first three measures of this "Ode to Joy" section are all quarter notes that get one beat each. Try it! Oddly enough, it was in May (May 7, 1824) that Beethoven's Symphony No. 9 was first performed, in Vienna. You might want to mention this fact.

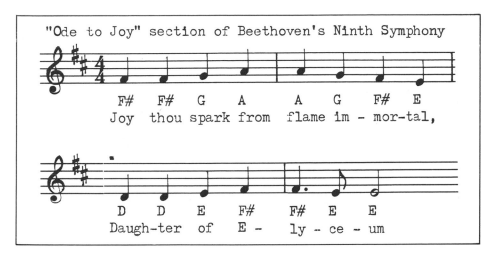

"Ode to Joy" section of Beethoven's Ninth Symphony

F# F# G A   A G F# E
Joy thou spark from flame im - mor-tal,

D   D   E   F#   F#   E   E
Daugh-ter of E - ly - ce - um

Figure 77

Bossa Novas of Brazil

Grades: 3-8.

Materials: Recording of bossa novas such as "Girl from Ipanema" and "Black Orpheus"; map of South America.

Concepts:

1. The dance and dance rhythm of the *bassa nova* came from Brazil.
2. Brazil is one of the larger countries in the world, and it is the largest country in South America.

Activities
&
Directions

1. Play a recording of Brazilian *bossa novas* and ask your students to guess which continent the music comes from. If they guess South America, set up the map of South America immediately. If they don't guess South America, ask them to choose between Africa and South America and then set up the map. After the map is set up, see if students can guess which country in South America the music comes from. If they don't guess it immediately, give them a hint by telling them that the language

used is Portuguese. Older students will probably guess after this hint, but if they don't you can tell them the country is Brazil at this point.

2. Ask students questions about the music such as: What types of instruments are being used? (Types of gourds, maracas, and drums are all acceptable answers—in addition to probable use of the guitar.) Is there a feeling of jazz in the music? (Answer should be yes, although not all musicians will agree.) Have students point to the large size of Brazil at the map.

Charleston Anyone?
(May 23)

Grades: K-8.

Materials: Recording of the Charleston (the dance); pictures of Charleston, South Carolina; map of the United States.

Concepts:

1. Not too many dances have been named after cities, but the Charleston is one.

2. The Charleston uses a syncopated figure of a dotted quarter note followed by an eighth note that is tied to a half note. (See Figure 78.)

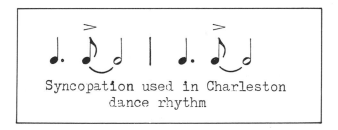

Syncopation used in Charleston dance rhythm

Figure 78

Activities
&
Directions

1. A background activity for this lesson can be locating South Carolina and the city of Charleston on the map or looking at pictures of the city of Charleston. You might ask your stu-

dents: "Is it a port city?" "How did it achieve its growth?" "Is it near any major rivers?" Tell students that South Carolina became a state on May 23, 1788.

2. The dance the Charleston has been defined as follows: "a fast fox-trot which drew its name from the South Carolina city and was first used in Negro revues, in New York 1922, to music by the Negroes Cecil Mack and Jimmy Johnson. During the next years it grew rapidly and took its place among the most popular numbers for ballroom dancing; but its popularity died out again just as quickly. The characteristic step consists of two twists on each foot with the other flung back convulsively." Why not play the recording and try to teach the dance to your students? Can you?

3. Place Figure 78 on the board and point out that the first note is a dotted quarter and that the second, an eighth note, is *tied* to the third, resulting in a *syncopation* or a displacement of the accent. Moreover, the second note is accented. The first two measures of the Charleston use this rhythm.

A Big State and a Little One
(May 29)

Grades: 2-8.

Materials: Map of the United States; some Wisconsin cheese; the Wisconsin Fight Song ("On Wisconsin"); Indian outfits or feathers; resonator bells.

Concepts:

1. There are many songs about states and many of them are college football songs.

2. Rhode Island is the smallest state; Wisconsin is among the larger of the 50 states.

3. A *sequence* is a melodic-rhythmic figure repeated at a higher or lower step.

**Activities
&
Directions**

1. Background activity for this lesson can be a comparison of the size and nature of Rhode Island and Wisconsin. For example,

Rhode Island is 49 by 37 miles; Wisconsin is 300 by 260 miles, or about six times as large. Rhode Island grew because of the hydro-electric power (water power) facilities of Providence. It is a hilly state with poor crops (Rhode Island ranks low agriculturally). Wisconsin is one of the best agricultural states, having more dairy cows and producing more milk, cheese, and butter than any other state. Rhode Island was admitted to the Union on May 29, 1790 and Wisconsin was admitted on May 29, 1848.

2. Since May includes "American Indian Day," you might want to try comparing the Indian names in Rhode Island (such as the Pawcatuck River and Narragansett Bay) with Indian names in Wisconsin (such as the Chippewa River). When Europeans discovered Wisconsin, it was the borderland between the hunting grounds of the Algonquian tribes and the Dakota or Sioux Indians. Even now there are Indian reservations in Wisconsin, with many members of the Chippewa, Menominee, Oneida, Winnebago, Munsee, and Stockbridge tribes living there.

3. Place Figure 79 on the chalkboard or on music flash cards. Circle the *sequences* as shown in Figure 79 and try to clap the rhythm. Can you guess what song it is? It is the Wisconsin Fight Song. Notice how there is a melodic-rhythmic figure in the first measure that is repeated in the second measure. Can you sing the words ("On Wis-con-sin, On Wis-con-sin, Fight to Victory")? Can you show your students how the melody goes up and then is repeated five times on the same note? Can you play it on the resonator bells? The notes are: G F♯ A G, C B D C, E E E E, E.

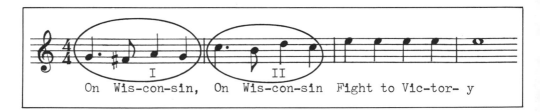

Figure 79

4. It might be fun to let younger students dress up like Indians (even though we often get overly selfconscious these days about activities that are considered to stereotype certain groups). Older students can do research on the Indian reservations in Wisconsin.

5. Of course, children young and old will probably enjoy some

delicious Wisconsin cheese. We think nothing tastes quite like it. Try it!

Happy Birthday Pete Seeger
(May 3)

Grades: 3-8.

Materials: Any recording of The Weavers, or of the many recordings made by Pete Seeger

Concepts:

1. So-called "folk singers" sing in many different languages and styles.
2. Pete Seeger is proficient on the banjo as well as the guitar.
3. The banjo is a traditional American instrument that originated in Africa.

**Activities
&
Directions**

1. Pete Seeger (born May 3, 1919) has made so many recordings that it is hard to know where to start. Both with The Weavers and alone he has sung hundreds and hundreds of songs in many different languages and styles. Your choice! Don't forget to point out the banjo if you choose one of his recordings where he is doing some good pickin' and strummin'.
2. If you're a "folk freak," why not discuss folk music. We've had success in comparing different folk singers such as Joan Baez, Judy Collins, and Burl Ives. You can also go back further to Woody Guthrie or even get into the controversy regarding Paul Robeson (who was born April 9, 1898).

COMPOSERS OF THE MONTH

Happy Birthday Tchaikovsky
(May 7)

Grades: 3-8.

Materials: Chalk and chalkboard; map of Europe; recording of the

1812 Overture by Tchaikovsky; recording of, or words and music for, the French national anthem.

Concepts:

1. In the 17th and 18th centuries, an overture was played at the beginning of a choral work, opera, and so on. Today (and in the case of the *1812 Overture*) an overture can be a composition by itself.

2. Peter Ilyitch Tchaikovsky was a Russian composer.

Activities & Directions

1. As a background activity, you might discuss briefly the War of 1812 that took place between France and Russia, including a discussion of the severe winters in Russia and how the French soldiers were affected by this weather. Can you compare that war with the American-British War of 1812? Or you can have pupils locate Paris and Moscow on the map.

2. Many music teachers teach their students the French national anthem prior to playing the *1812 Overture* so that they will be able to recognize it in the music when the recording is played. When you play the recording, another approach is to differentiate between the Russian church hymn and the French national anthem in the music. Another enjoyable approach is to listen for the cannons that are used in the music. Does your recording use real cannons, or are the cannons imitated by bass drums and tympani?

3. Place on the board:

   HAPPY BIRTHDAY TCHAIKOVSKY
   (May 7, 1840)

Figure 80

For pure fun, sing "Happy Birthday Peter Ilyitch," which should make your students giggle. You can also associate the most familiar part (see Figure 80) with the various commercials that have used the theme.

Brahms's Birthday
(May 7)

Grades: 4-8.

Materials: Recordings of any of Brahms's four symphonies; Recording of Brahms's *Academic Festival Overture* or a recording of Brahms's "Hungarian Dance Number 5"; a graduation gown and cap; map of Europe.

Concepts:

1. Along with Haydn, Mozart, and Beethoven, Brahms was one of the great composers of symphonies although he wrote only four of them.

2. When people graduate from a school they usually wear a cap and gown, and it is a very festive occasion.

**Activities
&
Directions**

1. On the chalkboard write:

   HAPPY BIRTHDAY JOHANNES BRAHMS
   (May 7, 1833—Hamburg, Germany)

   and either sing "Happy Birthday" or celebrate the occasion by eating hamburgers in honor of Brahms's birthplace. If you are singing "Happy Birthday," try leaving out "dear" and singing "Hap-py Birth-day Jo-han-nes." By the way, in German Johannes means John. Are there any Johns in your class who have just or are soon celebrating their birthdays? Point out that Brahms was born exactly 7 years before Tchaikovsky.

2. For delightful listening, you might listen to the first movement of the Third or Fourth Symphony by Brahms or the last movement of the First Symphony. If you want to start with something more familiar, try his "Hungarian Dance Number 5."

3. Fourth and fifth graders might like thinking ahead to their graduation. Have one or more children dress up as though they were graduating from high school or college, and with Brahms's *Academic Festival Overture* as background music, go through a mini-ceremony of getting a diploma.

Happy Birthday William Grant Still
(May 11)

Grades: 3-8.

Materials: Recordings of compositions by William Grant Still such as *Lenox Avenue Blues; Ennanga,* for harp, strings, and piano; *Danzas de Panama,* for string quartet; *Festive Overture,* for orchestra; *Darker America,* for orchestra; *Africa,* for orchestra; and his *Afro-American Symphony.*

Concept: William Grant Still, although working in the jazz field (several works were commissioned by Paul Whiteman) and writing music for Warner Brothers Hollywood films, was among America's great black American classical composers.

**Activities
&
Directions**

1. Place on the chalkboard:

   HAPPY BIRTHDAY WILLIAM GRANT STILL
   (May 11, 1895)

   You might provide your students with background about William Grant Still. He was born in Woodville, Mississippi, and studied in Little Rock, Arkansas, as well as at Wilberforce University and Oberlin College.

2. *Lenox Avenue* was commissioned by the Columbia Broadcasting System in 1937. Will your pupils know that Lenox Avenue is a street in Harlem or that Harlem is in New York City?

3. We hope you can locate a recording of *Darker America, Africa,* or *Afro-American Symphony.* They are among the works by William Grant Still that most clearly show his attempt to have his music reflect his African roots. However, these recordings have not been released lately, and if an extensive record library

does not contain copies, you may have to use materials that have been rerecorded in recent years (see "Materials").

Happy Birthday Sir Arthur Sullivan
(May 13)

Grades: K-8.

Materials: Recording of the overture to *Pirates of Penzance;* words or music to the song "Hail, Hail, the Gang's All Here"; songflute or songflutes; toy sword for a "knighting ceremony."

Concepts:

1. Together with W. S. Gilbert, Sir Arthur Sullivan was a great composer of comic operettas.
2. Half notes, dotted quarter notes, quarter notes, and eighth notes.
3. The songflute is an "easy-to-play" classroom instrument.

**Activities
&
Directions**

1. Background activity for this lesson might include a discussion of why Arthur Sullivan (born May 13, 1842) became Sir Arthur (no, not King Arthur, if some of your students confuse the two). It might even be fun to go through the knighting ritual or to discuss King Arthur and the Knights of the Round Table, referring perhaps to Mark Twain's delightful satire *A Connecticut Yankee in King Arthur's Court.*

2. If you play the overture to *Pirates of Penzance,* how many of your students will recognize the melody and start singing "Hail, Hail, the Gang's All Here"? (See Figure 81.) If none do, teach the song to them. You might also point out the half notes, dotted quarter note, quarter notes, and eighth notes in the figure. To assist you, we've labeled the half notes "H," the dotted quarter note "DQ," the quarter notes "Q," and the eighth note "Ei." Using Figure 81, you might remind students that if the bottom number of the time signature is four, a half note receives two beats, a dotted quarter receives one and a

half beats, a quarter note receives one beat, and an eighth note receives half of a beat. Have students come up to the board counting ONE two, ONE two, ONE two and point to the notes as you and the class sing "Hail, Hail, the Gang's All Here." Some students can sing, others can count, others can point.

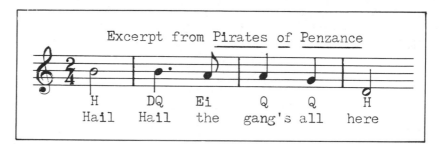

Figure 81

3. The songflute is a simple instrument that many music teachers have found easy to play and easy to teach. Figure 82 shows the fingering pattern for the first four measures of "Hail, Hail, the Gang's All Here." You should find this fun!

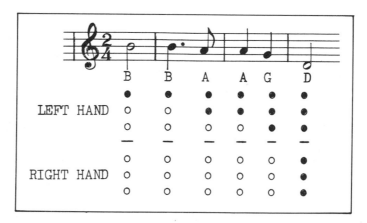

Figure 82

10

JUNE

Well! June is finally here. June is busting out all over; and there are more "June tunes"; and young children find June bugs fascinating. And even more important, some students are thinking about graduation, while others are thinking about what they'll do on vacation. Indeed, graduation and vacation—as good a rhyme as June, tune, and moon. How many hundreds of tunes from Tin Pan Alley were based on June and moon?

You can't ask for too many more major composers: Sir Edward Elgar, Aram Khatchaturian, Robert Schumann, Cole Porter, Carlos Chavez, Robert Russell Bennett, Edvard Grieg, and Richard Rogers. And let's not forget the famous folksinger-actor Burl Ives. (Any one of many songs sung by Burl Ives is enough to make you want July 1st to be around the corner; for example, "Jimmy Crack Corn and I Don't Care.")

Add to this all the states that became states in June—Kentucky, Arkansas, New Hampshire, and Virginia—and there is a considerable amount of material for delightful musical activities. For good measure, throw in Flag Day and Fathers Day and we have an abundance of music that can be used in the classroom.

Try to keep your eye on the ball though, so to speak, because your students will be thinking about July 1 from June on. Perhaps you will, too!

June

Figure 83

Grades: 1-8.

Materials: Music flash cards; music dictionaries or encyclopedias.

Concepts:

    1. A sixteenth note has two flags; a thirty-second note has three.

    2. Any letter of the alphabet can open up a world of music.

Activities
&
Directions

    1. Place Figure 83 on the chalkboard or music flash cards. Ask younger students what letter the month of June starts with. After getting the correct answer, J, ask your students to think of any music, singers, songs, and so on whose names start with the letter J. To ones that they think of, you might add Mozart's *Jupiter* Symphony (as his Symphony in C Major has come to be known). This symphony might provide a good listening activity, or you can start a dicussion of the planets—Jupiter,Mars, and so on—and how they were named after Roman gods.

    2. Have we discussed sixteenth notes yet? If you have not come across them in our lessons, why not point them out to your students in our diagram for June (see Figure 83). We have found that children are always fascinated by the flags on single sixteenth, thirty-second, and sixty-fourth notes. Explain that the number of flags determines the value of the note: one flag for an eighth, two flags for a sixteenth, three flags for a thirty-second, and so on (see Figure 84).

**Eighth,
Sixteenth,
Thirty-second
and
Sixty-fourth
notes.**

Figure 84

Tennessee and Kentucky
(June 1)

Grades: 1-8.

Materials: Words and music or a recording of "My Old Kentucky Home" by Stephen Foster and the "Tennessee Waltz"; music flash cards; bluegrass music.

Concepts:

1. C, D, E is *Do, Re, Mi* (C is *Do*, D is *Re*, E is *Mi*)
2. The "Tennessee Waltz" is in 3/4 meter, while "My Old Kentucky Home" is in 4/4 meter.

**Activities
&
Directions**

1. In honor of Tennessee and Kentucky achieving statehood on June 1st (in 1796 and 1792, respectively), you might listen to or sing the "Tennessee Waltz" and "My Old Kentucky Home." You might like to be more analytical and show (see Figure 85) that both songs start with the same three notes (*Do, Re, Mi*).

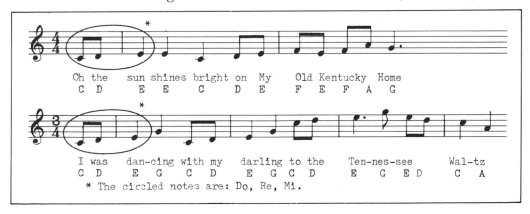

Figure 85

2. A simpler activity might be to listen to the bluegrass music of your choice. Some teachers assign older students to give reports on what bluegrass music is and how it differs from other country and western styles.

June Tunes
(First Week in June)

Grades: 3-8.

Materials: Chalk and chalkboard; recording of "Shine on Harvest Moon" or any songs (recordings or words and music) with *moon* or *June* in them.

Concepts:

1. Many songs have been written about June and many songs have June in the title.
2. Some songs about the moon have June as one of the words that rhymes with moon.

Activities
&
Directions

1. Ask students if they know any songs about June, such as "June Is Bustin' Out All Over." You and the students can list on the chalkboard as many songs as you can think of with June in the title or as one of the words that rhyme with *moon*. Then you might play a recording of "Shine on Harvest Moon," asking students to raise their hands as soon as they hear the word June. Or you can play other songs with *moon* or *June* in the title, such as "By the Light of the Silvery Moon." (See Figure 86.) Can you think of others?

Figure 86

2. Another enjoyable activity might be to discuss the question of why more modern popular songs don't use simple and obvious rhyming schemes such as "moon," "June," and "soon." Are songs getting more sophisticated? Or are there many popular songs that use this kind of rhyme scheme. This might be an interesting research project, particularly with older students.

3. You might want to teach the *tie* in music (see Figure 86). A *tie* is used to connect the whole note and the quarter note ("Light" and "of"), which are the third and fourth notes of the song "By the Light of the Silvery Moon."

Flag Day and National Flag Week (June 14 and by Proclamation)

Grades: K-8.

Materials: Flags or pictures of flags; recordings of patriotic songs such as "God Bless America" and "You're a Grand Old Flag"; recordings of patriotic compositions such as John Philip Sousa's "Stars and Stripes Forever" and Charles Ives's "Variations on America."

Concepts:

1. A presidential proclamation is issued each year for Flag Day—June 14.

2. The Bicentennial (200th anniversary of the United States) saw particular emphasis given to a National Flag Week.

**Activities
&
Directions**

1. In honor of Flag Day and National Flag Week, you might listen to or sing "God Bless America" and "You're a Grand Old Flag." (See Figure 87.)

2. Related discussion can center around our nation's history and June 14th being the day of the first flag of the United States. Many music teachers mention George M. Cohan, who made "You're a Grand Old Flag" famous, Irving Berlin, who wrote "God Bless America," and Kate Smith, who made the most famous recording of "God Bless America."

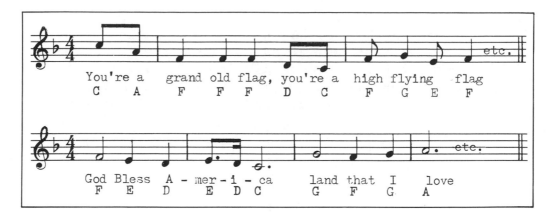

Figure 87

Birth of Burl: Happy Birthday Burl Ives
(June 14)

Grades: 2-8.

Materials: Recordings by Burl Ives (including "Jimmy Crack Corn" and "On Top of Old Smokey").

Concepts:

1. Some folk singers become radio, television, or Hollywood personalities.
2. Burl Ives's voice is considered to have a *tenor* quality.

**Activities
&
Directions**

1. Place on the chalkboard:

   BIRTH OF BURL or HAPPY BIRTHDAY BURL
   (June 14, 1909)

   Some students will enjoy the rhyme. You can sing "Happy Birthday," mention that for many years he was considered among America's finer folk singers, and point out that he was born on National Flag Day. He made many recordings, and you shouldn't have difficulty finding one that contains songs your students will enjoy. We have had great success with "Jimmy Crack Corn" and "On Top of Old Smokey."

2. Have you ever seen Burl Ives in a movie? Can you name one or two? Can your students name one or two that they have seen? Have any been on television? These questions can lead to a discussion of folk (or country and western) singers becoming radio, television, or Hollywood personalities. Others include Glen Campbell and Joan Baez. Try to discuss and list others.

3. Have you ever discussed voice quality with your students? Burl Ives's voice has a fairly high *tenor* quality. His voice can be compared with other famous folk singers such as Pete Seeger (whose voice is high but not as high) and Paul Robeson (who had a very deep *bass* voice).

Arkansas Traveller
(June 15)

Grades: 2-8.

Materials: Recording of "Arkansas Traveller" or other square dance music; chalk and chalkboard.

Concepts:

1. On June 15, 1838, Arkansas was admitted as a state.

2. The "Arkansas Traveller" is a traditional dance tune often said to be an "old world traditional dance tune in American form."

**Activities
&
Directions**

1. We have given you information on some states' famous colleges, railroads, and agricultural products, so you might start off this lesson by giving facts about Arkansas or by students giving reports on Arkansas. You can also look at a map to identify famous cities (such as Little Rock) and discuss things that may have happened in these cities. Can you think of something that happened in Little Rock regarding civil rights? Are there famous rivers in Arkansas? Lakes? On what states does it border? How many years before the beginning of the Civil War was Arkansas admitted as a state?

2. Why not have a square dance in your class! "Arkansas Traveller" is one of the many traditional tunes that is usually played
   on a fiddle or banjo to accompany a square dance. Similar
   songs are "Mississippi Sawyer" and "Turkey in the Straw."
   Since June also saw Virginia admitted as a state *almost exactly 50
   years earlier,* perhaps some older students might take on the
   challenge of investigating why the *Virginia Reel* is listed as a
   country dance rather than a square dance. Do you know the
   difference? (The *Virginia Reel* sometimes appears as part of
   square dance figures in play-party games such as "Bow, Bow,
   O Belindy.") Can you and your students list another five or six
   songs used for square dances?

Father's Day
(Third Sunday in June)

Grades: K-8.

Materials: Construction paper to make cards for Father's Day; recording of "Oh My Papa"; photographs that children have taken
of their fathers; Swiss Melode Bells.

Concepts:

1. On Father's Day, children give presents to their fathers or
   make cards for them in school (as well as buying cards in the
   store).

2. There are fewer songs in honor of Father's Day than for
   Mother's Day; the best known is "Oh My Papa."

Activities
&
Directions

1. Prior to making Father's Day cards from colored construction
   paper, we've had great success in motivating students to take
   pictures of their fathers or use pictures that they already have.
   Younger children, in particular, take great delight in making
   cards that use photographs of their fathers.

2. With older students, you might want to point out that the first
   five notes or tones of "Oh My Papa" are the same. We have
   written the beginning of this melody in F Major (see Figure 88)
   so that you can play it easily on the Swiss Melode Bells (which

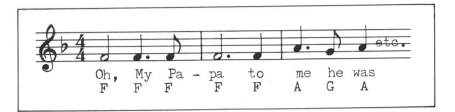

Figure 88

are probably the cheapest of the easy-to-play classroom instruments).

Nothing for New Hampshire?
(June 21)

Grades: 4-8.

Materials: Map of the United States; as many resources as possible to try to find songs about New Hampshire; recording of "Chicago, Chicago, a Wonderful Town."

Concepts:

1. New words can often be put to old songs.
2. New Hampshire is a beautiful state that many children would love to spend their summers in. It was the ninth state to ratify the Constitution, on June 21, 1788.

**Activities
&
Directions**

1. Now that you and your students are beginning to feel the intense summer heat, you might want to think about spending some time in some delightfully cool mountains. Using a map of the United States, you can point out the White Mountains of New Hampshire. Tell students that some of New Hampshire is pollen free, that it is a vacation paradise, and that (like Vermont) it is a state that produces delicious maple syrup. Perhaps you can give your students some delicious maple candies!
2. If you live in New Hampshire or attended Dartmouth college you might know the state song (Is there one?) or the

Dartmouth College football team song. But we have not been able to find them in our research. Unlike some of the better-known college and state songs ("Minnesota March On" or "On Wisconsin," for example) they are not well known. So here's an idea: Why not try to write a song about New Hampshire? Can you write one that will compare with "Moon Over Miami" or "Moonlight in Vermont"? You can use the music to "Chicago, Chicago, a Wonderful Town" and start off with the words "New Hampshire, New Hampshire, a Wonderful State." You can describe Mount Washington in the song or the many lakes, ponds, and streams that make the state so beautiful.

3. If all else fails, and for older children, why not play Schubert's "Trout" Quintet (Op. 114, in A Major) for the trout fishermen who would love to be fishing in New Hampshire.

Virginia Reel
(June 25)

Grades: 2-8.

Materials: Map of the United States; recordings of tunes used for the Virginia Reel, such as "Bow, Bow, O Belindy"; a book that explains specific steps for American country dances such as square and round dances.

Concepts:

1. The Virginia Reel can be a separate dance or part of square dance figures.

2. Virginia is one of the original 13 states. It became a state on June 25, 1788.

Activities
&
Directions

1. Teach the Virginia Reel to your class. Of course, you might have to learn it yourself first. But it is great fun and will be worth the effort. Do you know the steps for the Virginia Reel? Can you assign some of your students to try to find out? Is there a dance teacher in your school or a physical education teacher who specializes in folk dances? If all else fails, to help celebrate the day on which Virginia became a state obtain a folk dance book that includes an explanation of how to do the

Virginia Reel. Many music teachers have found that there is one readily available in their own school library or their local public library.

2. Before or after doing the Virginia Reel, use a map of the United States to locate the state of Virginia, bordering states, famous cities, famous rivers, and so on.

3. Another enjoyable activity might be to pay tribute to Southern hospitality. It used to be said that gentlemen from Virginia had the most perfect manners. We find such statements in the history books, on the recording of the Broadway musical *1776,* in the *Adams Chronicles,* and in papers written by Hamilton and Jefferson. Why not have a debate on this topic? Younger students might like to have a play in which they try to act out Southern hospitality and perfect manners.

FAIRS AND FESTIVALS

America has been called a "melting pot"; it is also said that we have "cultural plurality." June is a time when many cities and states begin to have fairs and festivals that honor ethnic minorities. In the next few pages we have listed and suggested materials and activities based on festivals in our country and abroad. We are sure you can find others. There are many musical moments that can be based on such fairs.

There are also other fairs that you can investigate to plan musical experiences. In the *Fiesta de San Antonio* there are ceremonial dances and Ghost Dances done by Tigua Indians. You might contact the Tigua Indian Reservation for more details. In Frankenmuth, Minnesota, there is a *Bavarian Festival* that features good food as well as traditional music (as it has been preserved in this country).

Of course, many of the jazz festivals start in June. The Hampton Jazz Festival in Hampton, Virginia, is one; the gigantic Newport Jazz Festival, originally in Newport, Rhode Island, and then in New York and Saratoga, is another. You can do your thing with "swing" music or any style of jazz. Why not jazz up June?

Country, Bluegrass, and Oldtime Fiddlin': International Country Music Fan Fair National Oldtime Fiddlers Contest & Festival Beanblossom Bluegrass Music Festival

Grades: K-8.

Materials: Potatoes; map of the United States; recordings of your choice of bluegrass music, country and western, or country style fiddling.

Concepts:

1. June is a month when there are many music fairs and festivals.
2. American folk music includes a distinctive "sound" of country fiddling and banjo playing.

Activities
&
Directions

1. Can your students find the city of Nashville and the state it is in? That's where every year there is an International Country Music Fan Fair. Can they find the city of Weiser (Idaho)? That's where they have a National Oldtime Fiddlers Contest and Festival. Can they find Martinsville (Indiana)? Every year Martinsville has a Beanblossom Bluegrass Music Festival where bluegrass greats gather to engage in pickin', strummin', and hummin'. These and other great festivals all take place in June. What a great month for the folk music of America!

2. Older students can investigate or discuss different styles of *pickin'* (using a pick or one finger or *strummin'* (using the whole hand). Younger children can play "Hot Potato" while listening to country fiddling to celebrate the Weiser, Idaho, National Oldtime Fiddlers Contest and Festival. As they play "Hot Potato," they can perceive the oldtime fiddling of pioneer America. We hope you can obtain the necessary recordings.

Swedes, Czechs and Danes

Grades: 2-8.

Materials: Recorded music of Scandinavia (Swedish and Danish dances might include *Yenta "O" Ja,* the *Cuckoo Waltz,* or *Janta Och Ja-Hambo*); Czechoslovakian polka music; compositions by Carl Nielsen, such as *Saga-Dream* and his Concerto for Clarinet.

Concepts:

1. June 6: June 6 is *Flag Day* in Sweden, which commemorates the day upon which Gustavus I ascended the throne of Sweden in 1523.

2. June 10: June 10-12 is a *Danish Festival* in Minden, Nebraska.

3. June 9: June 9, 1865, the Danish composer Carl Nielson was born at Lyndelse, Denmark.

4. June 17-19: *Swedish Festival* in Stromsburg, Nebraska.

5. June 20-21: *Czech Days Festival* in Tabor, South Dakota.

**Activities
&
Directions**

1. June is a festive month! Even a small town such as Tabor, South Dakota throws a gala celebration to honor its Czechoslovakian heritage—including singing, dancng, and polka music. What a marvelous time your pupils will have if you can treat them to some *Kolaches* (Czech fruit-filled pastries) while they listen to Czech polkas. Are there any students of Czechoslovakian descent in your class?

2. Nebraska has both a Danish Festival (in Minden) and a Swedish Festival (in Stromsburg). Perhaps your students can try to find the cities on a map while traditional polkas and mazurkas are played. If you locate recordings that have both *Yenta "O" Ja* and *Janta Och Ja-Hambo,* you can point out that they start almost exactly the same. (See Figure 89.)

Figure 89

**A Portuguese Holiday:
Camoes Memorial Day
(June 10)**

Grades: 3-8.

Materials: Map of Europe and world map; recording of the song "Lisbon Antigua" (In Old Lisbon) or the music; history books dealing with the Age of Exploration and Discovery; bossa novas of your choice or authentic Portuguese music.

Concepts:

1. June 10 is a national holiday in Portugal, commemorating the death of Portugal's national poet, Luis Vas de Camoes, who died in Lisbon on June 10, 1580.

2. "Lisbon Antigua" is a song about one of the cities considered among the most beautiful in the world.

**Activities
&
Directions**

1. Look at tiny Portugal on the map of Europe, a small strip adjacent to Spain. How is it that, at one time, Portugal controlled such vast areas of the world? You might discuss the Age of Discovery and the role of Vasco da Gama and the Portuguese fleet in exploring Africa. Can your students find the countries that were part of the empire Portugal controlled? What other countries were there besides Angola and Brazil?

2. Now for the effect of the music of Portugal. To what extent did Portuguese music affect the *bossa nova*? The words are Portuguese. Many music teachers point out that the Brazilian *bossa novas* are an amalgam of African, Brazilian Indian, and Portuguese influence. Another enjoyable activity is to listen to *bossa novas* of your choice or a recording of exciting authentic Portuguese music.

3. The song "Lisbon Antigua" (In Old Lisbon) can be played easily. Try the beginning. (See Figure 90.)

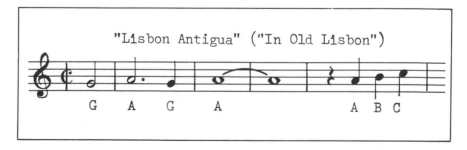

Figure 90

Kamehameha Day: Hawaiian Holiday
(June 11)

Grades: K-5.

Materials: Recordings of Hawaiian music; leis; pictures of Honolulu, Pearl Harbor, and other parts of Hawaii.

Concepts:

1. Kamehameha Day is a Hawaiian state holiday honoring the 18th century Hawaiian King Kamehameha 1, who was the first to rule over all of the islands.

2. Many children enjoy doing the hula, and every few years Hula-Hoops are popular with children.

Activities
&
Directions

1. On Kamehameha Day in Hawaii you'll find parades, pageantry, and luaus. Why not celebrate this day in your classroom? It might be fun. You could show pictures of Hawaii, discuss how it is a tropical paradise, and locate its major cities on a map. On the more serious side, you might mention Pearl Harbor and the start of World War II for the United States in the Pacific.

2. Using leis and recorded music of Hawaii, your students can do the hula. Do any of your pupils have Hula-Hoops?

3. There are many *standards* (popular songs that have gone into the repertory) about Hawaii. Many people know the "Hawaiian Wedding Song." Can you teach a little of "Hawaiian Paradise" to your pupils? (See Figure 91.)

Figure 91

If Your Thing Is Yodelling . . .
Northwest Swiss Yodelling Festival

Grades: K-5.

Materials: Map of Europe; Swiss cheese; recording of Swiss yodelling.

Concepts:

1. Every year in Switzerland they have a North-West Swiss Yodelling Festival.
2. The Swiss Alps are considered among the most beautiful mountains in the world.
3. Yodelling is a type of folk music that is perpetuated in Switzerland. There are many places in the United States where yodelling is done at country music festivals.

Activities
&
Directions

1. Many music teachers have found that young children are stimulated and amused by yodelling. It makes for a lot of fun to play recorded examples of yodelling, either the Swiss style or as it exists in America.
2. Is it hot enough (now that it is June) for you to wish you were skiing in the Swiss Alps? With a recording of Swiss yodelling in the background, you might have students locate the Swiss Alps on a map of Europe and discuss how they are still one of the skiing centers of the world.
3. Perhaps you live in a part of the country where yodelling is popular. Now that June is here, there are many parts of the country where there are country music festivals (e.g., Nashville: International Country Music Fan Fair; Martinsville: Beanblossom Bluegrass Music Festival). Can you and your students name others?
4. Just for a *percept,* play some yodelling and distribute small pieces of Swiss cheese. It will be a big hit with the young children. You might even ask kindergarten or first grade students if they know which cheese has holes in it before you give them this little snack. (For homonymn lovers, cheese with *holes* can be compared to *whole* notes regarding spelling.)

Scenes from Childhood:
Happy Birthday Robert Schumann
(June 8)

Grades: 3-8.

Materials: Chalk and chalkboard; record player; recording of Schumann's *Scenes from Childhood (Kinderscenen,* Op. 15), preferably the one by Horowitz, Columbia MS 6411.

Concept: Many composers have composed music about or specifically for children.

**Activities
&
Directions**

1. Place on the chalkboard:

   HAPPY BIRTHDAY ROBERT SCHUMANN
   June 8, 1810

   You might sing "Happy Birthday" or ask your pupils how many years ago Schumann was born (correlation with mathematics). Ask students if they can guess where Schumann was born. (Answer: Zwickau, Saxony, which is now part of Germany.) We've used this question to lead into a discussion of the unification of Germany, the two World Wars, and the division of Germany again. Another background activity might be explaining the tragedy of Schumann, who suffered from insanity for most of his life and finally tried to commit suicide by throwing himself into the Rhine River. He died shortly thereafter.

2. Place the titles of the individual piano pieces in *Scenes from Childhood* on the chalkboard (asking the children if the music sounds very much like the titles or only a little bit):

   (1) From foreign lands and peoples
   (2) A curious story
   (3) Blind man's bluff
   (4) Pleading child
   (5) Perfect happiness
   (6) An important event
   (7) Dreaming (*Traumeri*)
   (8) At the fireside
   (9) Knight of the hobby horse
   (10) Almost too serious

(11) Frightening
(12) Child falling asleep
(13) The poet speaks

OTHER COMPOSERS OF THE MONTH

In many parts of the country, June is a very short school month for children—and how they must love it—because schools recess so that important agricultural tasks can be taken care of. Yet there were so many important composers born in June! Here are some short lesson ideas for what might be for you a short month.

Grades: 2-8.

Concept: Any day can be the birthday of an important composer.

Happy Birthday Sir Edward Elgar
(June 2)

Materials: Any of the "Pomp and Circumstance" marches and the *Enigma Variations*.

**Activities
&
Directions**

1. Place on the board:

   HAPPY BIRTHDAY SIR EDWARD ELGAR
   June 2, 1857

   Sing Happy Birthday.

2. Practice graduation marching to the traditional "Pomp and Circumstance" Marches. If your pupils are not graduating (or don't want to march) they can try to figure out the puzzle in the *Enigma Variations* (What is the enigma?).

Happy Birthday Aram Khachaturian
(June 6)

Materials: Recorded excerpts from the *Gayne* ballet suite; map of Europe.

**Activities
&
Directions**

1. Place on the board:

    HAPPY BIRTHDAY ARAM KHACHATURIAN
    June 6, 1903

    Sing Happy Birthday.

2. Find Armenia on the map (Khachaturian was born there) and listen to the well-known and exciting "Russian Saber Dance." Use plastic sabers if you can obtain them to re-enact what you think the dance would be like.

Happy Birthday Cole Porter
(June 9)

Materials: Recordings of "Begin the Beguine" or "Night and Day" or the score from *Kiss Me Kate*.

**Activities
&
Directions**

1. Place on the board:

    HAPPY BIRTHDAY COLE PORTER
    June 9, 1893

    Sing Happy Birthday.

2. A beguine is like a rhumba. Can you demonstrate it for your students? You might try doing the rhumba to Cole Porter's well-known "Begin the Beguine." "Night and Day" is another one of his famous songs that has been recorded by many singers. We suggest the Frank Sinatra version. If you have time for an entire score, many music teachers have found that *Kiss Me Kate* (the Broadway musical that was based on Shakespeare's *The Taming of the Shrew*) makes for enjoyable listening. We have found that some students find it amusing to learn that Cole Porter was born in Peru—but not Peru, South America, Peru, Indiana!

Happy Birthday Carlos Chavez
(June 13)

Materials: Recorded examples of music by Carlos Chavez such as *Sinfonia India* or *Toccata for Percussion*; see the lesson on the Mexican holiday *Dia de la Candelaria* in Chapter 6; map of Central America.

**Activities
&
Directions**

1. Place on the board:

    HAPPY BIRTHDAY CARLOS CHAVEZ
    June 13, 1899

    Sing Happy Birthday.

2. Background activities for this lesson can include doing the Mexican hat dance or looking at pictures of Mexico and discussing the conquest of the Aztecs. Carlos Chavez was a Mexican composer. Pupils are often surprised to learn that the *Sinfonia India* is neither about the country of India nor about American Indians. Take a few moments, perhaps, to think about the Mexican Indians (and movies that have been inspired by the Mexican liberation from the yoke of Spain and later France). *Toccata for Percussion* is another Chavez composition that is very exciting and is used by many music teachers.

Happy Birthday Robert Russell Bennett
(June 15)

Materials: Recordings of compositions by Robert Russell Bennett: *Commemoration Symphony* ("Stephen Foster"), *Symphonic Story of Jerome Kern*, *Suite of Old American Dances*; arrangements by Robert Russell Bennett of compositions by Richard Rodgers.

**Activities
&
Directions**

1. Place on the board:

HAPPY BIRTHDAY ROBERT RUSSELL BENNETT
June 15, 1894

Sing Happy Birthday.

2. Many of Richard Rodgers' Broadway musicals were scored for orchestra by Robert Russell Bennett. Music teachers have been fond of pointing this out to students. Yet he was a talented composer as well as an orchestrator. You might explain that an orchestrator often takes music that has been written for the piano and writes it out so that a full orchestra can play it. It is interesting that both Bennett and Rodgers were born in June. You can play Robert Russell Bennett's original compositions or his orchestrations of Richard Rodgers' Broadway scores.

Happy Birthday Edvard Grieg
(June 15)

Materials: Map of Europe; recordings of compositions by Edvard Grieg (such as his *Norwegian Dances*, the well-known *Peer Gynt Suite*, Op. 46, and the incidental music from *Peer Gynt*); translated copy of the play *Peer Gynt* by Ibsen.

**Activities
&
Directions**

1. Place on the board:

   ## HAPPY BIRTHDAY EDVARD GRIEG
   ### June 15, 1843

   Sing Happy Brithday.

2. As background for this lesson, pupils can locate Norway on a map of Europe. You might also point out that on June 15 in Norway there are special celebrations at Lofthus on the Hardanger Fjord, where Grieg's cabin still stands. Students can figure out that Grieg was born exactly 51 years before Robert Russell Bennett. Now for the music. What a month for Scandinavian music! There are Swedish and Danish festivals in Nebraska (as well as in Sweden and Denmark) and the birthday of the composer who wrote one of the pieces that children all used to know—*Peer Gynt*. How can children grow up never having heard "Morning Mood" or "In the Hall of the Moun-

tain King" from the incidental music that Grieg wrote for Ibsen's play? Well, they won't miss it if they have *you* as a teacher—right?

Happy Birthday Richard Rodgers
(June 28)

Materials: Recording of *South Pacific*, *Oklahoma*, *The King and I*, *Carousel*, or *Victory at Sea*; any pictures that might relate to the music you choose to use (e.g., ships at battle, Siam, and so on).

**Activities
&
Directions**

1. Place on the board:

   HAPPY BIRTHDAY RICHARD RODGERS
   June 28, 1902

   Sing Happy Birthday.

2. If your school district does not end school in the middle of June, June 28 should certainly be one of the last, if not the last, days of school. As much as we all love school, we must admit that we look forward to the summer at this time of the year. The weather is so beautiful! Why not Rexograph the words to "Oh What a Beautiful Morning" or write them on the chalkboard?

   > "Oh what a beautiful morning
   > Oh what a beautiful day
   > I've got a beautiful feeling
   > Everything's going my way"

   Another song that children relate to very well is "Dites-moi," from *South Pacific*. See the lesson on French Conversation Week in Chapter 4 for the words. Still another song from a Richard Rodgers score that is particularly relevant to children is the "March of the Siamese Children" from *The King and I*.

3. Another enjoyable activity for young children is to listen to the score from *Victory at Sea* (which was written for the television series that is re-run every so often) while playing with toy ships (cruisers, battle ships, torpedo boats, and so on). We have had great success with this activity.

4. The music to *Carousel* makes one think of the outdoors and the fun we can have in the summer. Many music teachers have found that it is well received.

What Will You Do This Summer?

Grades: 3-8 (or 2-8).

Materials: Travel posters; travelogues.

Concepts:

1. In the summer, concerts come to you.
2. In the summer, as well as in June, there are many country, folk, jazz, and classical music festivals.

**Activities
&
Directions**

1. At some point during June, you can discuss what musical events students will participate in or attend during the summer. Among the discussions can be ones about:
   a. Concerts in the park
   b. Promenade concerts
   c. Summer jazz festivals
   d. Summer folk festivals
   e. Summer country and western festivals
2. Travelogues might be shown that include exotic music of foreign countries.